The Sign of the Swan

Frontispiece. Édouard Manet, Stéphane Mallarmé (1842–98), poet, in 1876, Musée d'Orsay, public domain image via Google Art Project / Wikimedia Commons

The Sign of the Swan

How French Symbolist Poetry Re-envisions Reality

William Franke

Anthem Press
An imprint of Wimbledon Publishing Company
www.anthempress.com

This edition first published in UK and USA 2026
by ANTHEM PRESS
75–76 Blackfriars Road, London SE1 8HA, UK
or PO Box 9779, London SW19 7ZG, UK
and
244 Madison Ave #116, New York, NY 10016, USA

Copyright © 2026 William Franke

The author asserts the moral right to be identified as the author of this work.

All rights reserved. Without limiting the rights under copyright reserved above, no part of this publication may be reproduced, stored or introduced into a retrieval system, or transmitted, in any form or by any means (electronic, mechanical, photocopying, recording or otherwise), without the prior written permission of both the copyright owner and the above publisher of this book.

British Library Cataloguing-in-Publication Data
A catalogue record for this book is available from the British Library.

Library of Congress Cataloging-in-Publication Data: 2026931260
A catalog record for this book has been requested.

ISBN-13: 978-1-83999-932-1 (Pbk)
ISBN-10: 1-83999-932-2 (Pbk)

Cover credit: Brian Stevens

This title is also available as an eBook.

Ce qu'il nous faut à nous, les Suprêmes Poètes
Qui vénérons les Dieux et qui n'y croyons pas,
À nous dont nul rayon n'auréola les têtes,
Dont nulle Béatrix n'a dirigé les pas,
               …
Ce qu'il nous faut à nous, c'est l'étude sans trêve,
C'est l'effort inouï, le combat nonpareil,
C'est la nuit, l'âpre nuit du travail, d'où se lève
Lentement, lentement, l'Œuvre, ainsi qu'un soleil !

     —Paul Verlaine, Épilogue, *Poèmes saturniens*
                                           (1866)

What is necessary for us, the Supreme Poets
Who venerate the Gods and who do not believe in them,
For us whose heads are haloed by no ray,
Whose steps are guided by no Beatrice
               …
What is necessary for us is study without ceasing,
Unheard of effort, incomparable combat,
The night, the harsh night of work, in which arises
Slowly, slowly, the Work, just like the sun!

CONTENTS

Preface	ix
Introduction: Baudelaire—Rimbaud—Mallarmé: Revolution and Revelation in Poetic Language	1
1. Making Beings Speak: The Linguistic Epistemology of French Symbolist Poetry	5
Intrinsic Meanings of Things Expressed through Symbols	10
The Pre-semiological and Sub-semantic	18
2. Illustrative Readings of Mallarmé's Poems as Symbolist Works	25
Sonnet en x ("Ses Purs Ongles")	26
Sonnet en i ("Le vierge, le vivace, et le bel aujourd'hui")	34
"L'après-midi d'un faune"	38
Undecidability Rather than Suppression of Reference	40
Meanderings of Chance from *Igitur* to *Un coup de dés*	43
3. Symbolist Meaning and Subjective Feeling	51
4. Mallarmé's Negative Poetics of De-Objectification through the Symbol	59
"L'après-midi d'un faune" Encore: From Representational Emptying to Verbal Presence	65
Speaking the Being of Language—Or Rather its Nothing	70
Concluding Reflection	73
Bibliography	75
Index	79

PREFACE

This concise book offers an introduction to reading some of the most beautiful, difficult, and influential poems of Stéphane Mallarmé (1842–98). The readings are encased within and take their cues from an original, philosophically grounded interpretation of the linguistic epistemology of French symbolist poetry. They probe the extraordinary ways in which poetic language becomes an instrument of otherwise inaccessible knowledge. The interpretations offered here aim to let the supreme sense of these poems sing out and shine through in the majestic splendor of their all too elusive and too seldom appreciated intelligibility. The understanding of these enigmatic poems is a first step toward appreciating the far-reaching creative project and cosmic vision of their author, as well as to fathoming the furthest potential of poetic language in general.

The poetry expounded here is the germ of a social and political revolution that is the subject of a companion volume entitled *Mallarmé's Theo-Political Poetics: Revolution and Revelation in French Symbolist Poetry* (Cambridge University Press, forthcoming in 2026). This follow-up volume emphasizes the intellectual debates generated around Mallarmé's extraordinary work in our own time, whereas the volume in hand focuses more directly on reading the poems and the distinctive intellectual and spiritual vision that they incarnate and inculcate. This introductory reading includes, naturally, an initiation into the requisite theoretical instruments and an orientation to the work's cultural-historical background.

All translations, unless otherwise attributed, are my own.

Villa Canta la Mar
Les Issambres, Roquebrune-sur-Argens
Le Var
France

Introduction

BAUDELAIRE—RIMBAUD—MALLARMÉ: REVOLUTION AND REVELATION IN POETIC LANGUAGE

These three poets—Baudelaire, Rimbaud, and Mallarmé—show up as leading beacons lighting the way to radical symbolist practices of poetry. All are resolutely modern and, as such, accept a secular worldview as given. However, they are also trenchantly anti-modern in many of their most tenacious convictions and characteristic orientations. They rebel against modern, mass, industrialized society and its crass, commercial materialism. They take refuge and find resources in poetry as an indispensable spiritual instrument and weapon for defying such a mechanical worldview and material culture. They use poetry as a means of negation, negation that can work powerfully as a ferment of social *revolution*. But poetry can also serve them in vital ways as a leaven for *revelation* in a quasi-religious sense. This equivocal revolution-cum-revelation takes place most radically at the level of poetic technique. With each of these three geniuses of poetic creativity, novel explorations of the capacities of language lead to experimental reinventions of the whole spectrum of language's awe-inspiring, wonder-provoking performances. As reinvented by these symbolist poets, poetic language envisions a revolution for political society and practically a mystical form of revelation of a spiritual vocation and potential for humanity.

Revolutionary about these three poets, among others, is that poetic language becomes revelatory again in their work in something of a religious, or at least a spiritual, sense. I say *again* because this movement commonly dubbed "symbolist" repeats numerous outgrowths of tradition with its roots in poetry since time immemorial. These perennial flourishings include the Orphic hymns in the classical, Greco-Roman world and the prophetic books of the Bible in the Judeo-Christian canon. Such a conception of poetry was still alive and thriving in the Middle Ages, notably in the form of dream visions revealing supernal or infernal realities. It was revived in important ways by these Symbolist poets and their Romantic forebears after being dealt nearly a deathblow by the pervasive mechanization and rationalization of modern industrial society.

Such pre-modern pasts of poetry are explicitly evoked by these poets living through and coping with the consequences of the modern industrial revolution. Employing, ironically, the rational and scientific idiom of "explication," Mallarmé writes of "the Orphic explanation of the universe" as the "only duty of the poet and the literary game par excellence" ("l'explication Orphique de la Terre, qui est le seul devoir du poète et le jeu littéraire par excellence").[1] Mallarmé also designated "destruction" as his "Beatrice,"[2] in an upending reference to Dante, who momentously united classical with biblical strands of revelation in poetry. Nevertheless, modern poets perform this re-actualization of the revelatory vocation of poetry from within a fully secularized outlook and ethos. They live in a world that has been stripped of its traditional religious meaning and enchantment, and they turn to poetry as the only viable means available to restore a measure of mystery and spiritual depth of symbolic meaning to human life.

Their most imposing poetic predecessor, Victor Hugo, had cast his poetic project in a prophetic mold (emblematically in "Les Mages" and in "Le promontoire du songe"). However, Hugo's prophetic air and manner are, for his symbolist successors, vestiges of a bygone era and a world already surpassed. In their prevailing judgment, Hugo reminisces more than he revolutionizes—at least as concerns specifically the poetic form and aspect of his literary *oeuvre*. He remains unwavering in his adherence to the classic French verse form, the alexandrine. The three poets featured here, in contrast, are situated along the axis of a new departure—leveraged especially from formal innovation—for a resolutely contemporary poetry. In both form (often ironic) and content (often contemporary), they place their prophetic and visionary writing on a new footing grounded within a modern, secular world. Rimbaud emphatically states: "It is necessary to be absolutely modern" ("Il faut être absolument moderne").[3]

And yet, these three "accursed" poets (*poètes maudits* in Paul Verlaine's telling phrase) are also in crucial respects aggressively anti-modern. They are reacting to a new historical situation. They find that they must recreate the institution of literature in a way that changes fundamentally its relation

---

[1] Letter to Paul Verlaine, November 16, 1885. Mallarmé's letters are quoted from *Œuvres complètes*, I, ed. Bertrand Marchal (Paris: Gallimard, 1998), 788.

[2] "La Destruction fut ma Béatrice." Letter to Eugène Lefébure, May 17, 1867, *Œuvres complètes*, I, 717.

[3] "Adieu," in *Une saison en enfer*. Arthur Rimbaud, *Complete Works, Selected Letters*, ed. Wallace Fowlie (Chicago: University of Chicago Press, 1966).

to the society into which it speaks. As a voice of revelation of a higher order of meaning and truth for these poets, poetry cannot but express itself in revolutionary terms because the modern world in which it exists no longer recognizes any such possibility as "revelation," at least not in the religious or miraculous sense associated with the Bible. The modern world that emerged from the eighteenth-century Enlightenment tended to reduce poetry to little more than versified prose. Alexander Pope's verse in rhyming couplets typifies this style of refined social discourse for many Anglophone readers. Nicolas Boileau's poetic work, especially his *Art poétique*, with its rationalizing and didactic alexandrines, furnishes a rough equivalent for the French. But revelatory poetry is a new and revolutionary creation in the conception of the epoch-making symbolist poets of modern France.[4] The revolution in poetic language—and the *revelation* from which it is inextricable—is bound up with a new approach to poetic figuration that turns especially on a particular, and a novel, conception of the symbol.

Preliminary to a theoretical elucidation of this new conception, a note concerning the historical development that gives it its impetus is in order. "Symbolisme" is a retrospective construction of a movement in literature that never existed as such in the consciousness of the primary *symboliste* masters, most often identified as Baudelaire, Rimbaud, Verlaine, and Mallarmé. In 1938, Paul Valéry ironically celebrated the "birth" of the movement at the mature age of fifty, having skipped all the difficulties of infancy and adolescence. He thereby exposed *symbolisme* as a retrospective construction: "We construct Symbolism; we cause it to be born today at the felicitous age of fifty years old" ("Nous construisons le Symbolisme; nous le faisons naître aujourd'hui à l'âge heureux de cinquante ans").[5]

About fifty years before Valéry's pronouncement, the remarkable year 1886 had seen the publication of Rimbaud's *Illuminations*, René Ghil's *Traité du Verbe*, with a preface by Mallarmé, and Jean Moréas's *Manifeste littéraire*. Valéry, looking back from his perspective with a half-century of historical distance, discerns the inchoate outlines of this literary movement that never existed as such. At least it had not been so identified by those who were to emerge later as its earliest protagonists and leading beacons, including Charles Baudelaire, who was recognized as progenitor and "phare" (beacon), to use

---

4 All these strands and their dialectical interaction are lucidly laid out by Paul Bénichou, *Le sacre de l'écrivain 1750–1830. Essai sur l'avènement d'un pouvoir spirituel laïque dans la France moderne* (Paris: Gallimard, 1996).

5 Paul Valéry, "Existence de symbolisme," *Œuvres*, I, ed. J. Hytier (Paris: Gallimard, 1957), 688.

his own language ("Les Phares").[6] Symbolism, since its inception, belongs thus in decisive and destiny-laden ways to the realm of theory. Theory will be unveiled here as its driving force and furnish the key to its elucidation. It is with Mallarmé and his theorization of poetic language that the thrust of symbolism reaches its acutest pitch and deepest penetration, as well as its highest degree of challenge and intelligibility.

---

[6] The formidable difficulties of identifying the referent for "symbolisme" are deftly parsed by Bertrand Marchal, *Le symbolisme* (Paris: Armand Colin, 2011). These difficulties, for Marchal, lead to Mallarmé's ideas on aesthetics, in which they are resolved.

Chapter 1

MAKING BEINGS SPEAK: THE LINGUISTIC EPISTEMOLOGY OF FRENCH SYMBOLIST POETRY

In the canonical definition and theory of the symbol forged early in the nineteenth century by, among others, Goethe and Coleridge, the symbolic is the preferred mode of figuration and is viewed rather mystically. In Goethe's words, the symbol is the "living momentary revelation of the inscrutable" ("lebendig-augenblickliche Offenbarung des Unerforschlichen").[1] Coleridge, not dissimilarly, views the symbolic as living, organic form because it requires no logical operations but constitutes simply the "unmediated vision" of the imagination. This justifies placing symbolic above allegorical forms of representation: "The advantage of symbolic writing over allegory is that it presumes no disjunction of faculties, but simple dominance."[2] A kind of immediacy of presence is achieved by means of the symbol that can transcend the normal limits of representation.

A mere (non-symbolic) representation, in contrast, is typically external to what it represents. It thus refers to something as a presence that is absent, absent from the *re*presentation and its referential mode of indicating or evoking what is *not* concretely and immediately present in the signifier (word or sign) itself. The preference for and exaltation of the symbol is symptomatic of impatience with the secondariness of representation and aims to reverse it into the primariness of real presence. Following this impulse, the founders of the movement later recognized and baptized as French symbolism (including Baudelaire, Rimbaud, Verlaine, and especially Mallarmé) began to focus on words and their constitutive linguistic elements as presences in their own right and not just as tokens able to stand for and represent something else.

---

1 Johann Wolfgang von Goethe, *Gedenkausgabe der Werke, Briefe und Gespräche*, ed. Ernst Beutler (Zürich and Stuttgart: Artemis Verlag, 1949), 9: 532.
2 Samuel Taylor Coleridge, *Miscellaneous Criticism*, ed. T. M. Raysor (London: Constable, 1936), 30. See, further, Geoffrey Hartmann, *The Unmediated Vision: An Interpretation of Wordsworth, Hopkins, Rilke, and Valéry* (New Haven: Yale University Press, 1954).

In symbolist aesthetics, the word had value—even multifarious values—already as a direct presentation of sound and visual form. The semantic value of words, as determined referentially by the system of conventional meanings, was demoted to secondariness and treated as outstripped by the meanings inherent in words and letters themselves as sensuous presences.

The physical qualities of words and their component syllables were themselves plumbed as eminently and superlatively meaningful. The sensory matter of the word, both auditory and visual, became the most significant aspect in determining its "symbolic" value for symbolists—or "symbolistes."[3] At least this concrete meaning as a sensuous presence was able to work in conjunction with the conventional senses of words in their dictionary meanings to inflect meaning—or to *de*flect it in some novel and unexpected directions. In effect, meaning was opened up to all the uncontainable determinations of any actual physical being.

While determined in certain specific ways *as* something, any real physical presence hosts an immeasurable density and a plenum of sensation that can never be adequately represented and totalized by any conceptual enumeration of characteristics. The physical being of things, including that of linguistic signs as physical marks, is already saturated with an untold sensory depth of being that abstract means of representation can never exhaust. This unlimited being and its infinite potential for meaning becomes primary for symbolist poets: it displaces the semantically determined and delimited meanings of words from their presumed centrality to the margins of meaning as being less rich and poetically potent than the word seen and heard concretely as a symbol.

It is customary to treat the symbolist aesthetic as privileging "connotative" over "denotative" meaning in the terms popularized by I. A. Richards and traceable to John Stuart Mill's logical works. Symbolism has also been characterized as revolving around "intraverbal" significance, in Northrop Frye's jargon.[4] Certainly, this designation, too, points out an important aspect of the symbolist shifting of the ground of language's meaning. But the change is even more fundamental than just an increased emphasis on

---

3 I often use "symboliste" as a more exact way of referring to the French symbolist poetry (and its epigones) that emerges in its specificity from a much larger field of symbolist or symbolic writing and art of many varied sorts and provenances in diverse epochs. I make an analogous distinction between *symbolisme* and "symbolism": the former term is historically specific to the literary movement originating in nineteenth-century France.

4 Both of these references are evoked by Robert G. Cohn, "Symbolism," *The Journal of Aesthetics and Art Criticism* 33/2 (1974): 181–92.

the broader "semantic fields" of words, which overlap and shade into those of others independently of objective referentiality and the practical function of language.

Symbolist poetry endeavors, more radically, to derive meaning from the form of words iconographically present on the page or physically sounded out in reading *regardless* of their semantic contents. At least, meaning derives from these concrete qualities rebounding back upon and bleeding into those semantic contents and coloring them anew. To a significant degree, this makes French symbolist poetry revolutionary, starting especially from the reputedly obscure and hermetic collage compositions of Mallarmé and the experimentations of Rimbaud, particularly in his *Illuminations*.

The material signifier signifies in symbolist fashion through a penumbra of suggestion based on sensuous impressions that exceed the limits of the signified as determined by the conceptual meaning the word bears. This fusion and thoroughgoing interpenetration of sensuous form and intellectual content in language is, arguably, essential to poetry per se. Linguist Roman Jakobson defined the "poetic function" of language as that of making sense sensuous, that is, of making intellectual meaning ("sense") palpable to the physical senses ("sensation").[5] From a linguistic, as well as a poetic, point of view, this capability of language reaches some of its most consciously programmatic realizations in the poetry and theory of the *symbolistes*.[6]

Such symbolist language is made to reflect on its own physical form. Nevertheless, the material signifiers in words do not only become objects in their own right, which would be simply to fetishize them. In that case, the signifiers and words of the poem, finally, would have no more interest or symbolic value than the material objects that they can evoke and relate to as their referents. It is only *within* the economy of the sign, or, better, of the figure (if, as I contend, ultimately signification is always dependent on some degree of figuration), that the excess created by the material signifier counts—or rather exceeds accountability into the incommensurable. The "normal" economy of the sign can be formulated as a simple exchange: *quid pro quo*. But the symbol changes this to a *quid pro toto*. Whatever serves as signifier can no longer be delimited in its signification but turns, instead, into an irreducibly particular way of signifying without limit. Such a signifier potentially signifies anything and *everything*, the whole world, or a totalized universe.

---

5 Roman Jakobson, "Linguistics and Poetics: Closing Statement," in *Style in Language*, ed. Thomas Sebeok (Cambridge: MIT Press, 1960), 373.

6 Bertrand Marchal's previously cited *Le symbolisme* expertly delineates the extension and intension of the term "symbolism."

Accordingly, symbolic significance, in the sense opened up by the *symbolistes*, has to be conceived of as a deflection from and deformation of ordinary dictionary sense. It entails a sliding away and a freeing from rigid and extra-linguistically determined referential significance. This alternative sort of significance has been theorized in psycholinguistic terms by Julia Kristeva in *La révolution du langage poétique* under the rubric of the semiotic ("le sémiotique").[7] This level of linguistic performance manifests psycho-physical "pulsions" or impulses through deformations of the regular structures of language. This amounts to another way of getting at real being, material and psychological, behind the artifices of language. Kristeva finds that this is exactly what poets like Mallarmé achieve by their *symboliste* technique. She finds a similar sort of revolution in poetic language in the work of Lautréamont (Isidore Lucien Ducasse, 1846–70), who was later taken as precursor and patron saint of the Dadaist movement in all its iconoclastic and revolutionary *élan*.

It should be noted, however, that Kristeva emphasizes perhaps somewhat one-sidedly the disruptive aspects of the semiotic, which is "indifferent to language" ("indifférent au langage"), allowing for no possibility of its being inherently disciplined and harmonious. The vision of the *symboliste* poets, in contrast, included an aspiration toward an ideal meaning and perfection. They were driven by desire for expression free from conventional codes so as to disclose an originary, ideal order. Mallarmé speaks almost obsessively of the "pure idea" and the ideal, and even Baudelaire had often composed with an ideal in mind of pure order and beauty, which was also sensual delight ("Là tout n'est qu'ordre et beauté / Luxe, calme et volupté," "L'invitation au voyage"). The dialectic of "Spleen et Idéal" (Spleen and Ideal) is foundational for his *Fleurs du mal* right from its opening and longest section.

Well before Walter Benjamin in "The Task of the Translator" ("Die Aufgabe des Übersetzers"), the introduction to his 1923 translation of Baudelaire's "Tableaux Parisiens," Mallarmé hypothesizes one pure language projected from the many diverse, historical languages. Benjamin himself takes Mallarmé as guide for his own exposition, citing the following passage from Mallarmé's "Crise de vers":

> Languages are imperfect by virtue of being many, in which they miss the supreme: since thinking is writing without accessories or whispering but rather tacit still the immortal word, diversity on earth of tongues prevents anyone from proffering the words that, otherwise, by a single stroke, would find materially the truth.

---

7 Kristeva, La révolution du langage poétique—*L'avant-garde à la fin du XIXe siècle: Lautréamont et Mallarmé* (Paris: Seuil, 1974).

Les langues imparfaites en cela que plusieurs, manque la suprême : penser étant écrire sans accessoires, ni chuchotement mais tacite encore l'immortelle parole, la diversité, sur terre, des idiomes empêche personne de proférer les mots qui, sinon se trouveraient, par une frappe unique, elle-même matériellement la vérité.[8]

Symbolist language works on such a logic of wholeness, whereby all things are intimately and internally related in a way that can evoke what Hegel called the "concrete universal."[9] Mallarmé, like Benjamin, was well aware of Hegel, "this miraculous genius."[10] The symbolist poets, however, take this cosmic vision of dialectical wholeness from the ontological register of philosophy to the specifically linguistic level and therewith open a new vista.

In symbolist language, there is an interpenetration or osmosis of the semiological and the phonemic into the conceptual that renders the ideality of meaning incarnate. The word has an ideal meaning by virtue of the concept it signifies, but at the same time, its effectual sense depends also on material elements that mean in ways exceeding control by concepts. This makes the word a material incarnation of a meaning which is not merely that of the concept but rather of an ideality suggesting further meanings—those evoked by the word as material signifier bearing infinite analogies with all other things. A word like "nue," which can mean either "cloud" or "nude," can become a cloudy manner of rather nakedly or nondescriptly designating anything whatsoever along multiple axes of meaning turning on its sound or iconographic form. The word thus becomes the realization of an infinite ideality concretely and essentially in a certain type of material thing, a "signifier." The material is essential in the evocation or "presencing" of the infinite ideality, which otherwise could never be comprehended, except abstractly in a concept.

This oscillation, or going back and forth between sense and sonority, constitutes their vibratory presence and characterizes words in their poetic or "essential" state as words of a verse. It is described by Mallarmé in "Crise de vers" as the "the artifice of their redunking alternately in sense and in sonority" ("l'artifice de leur retrempe alternée dans le sens et la

---

8 Mallarmé's criticism and poems are quoted from Mallarmé, *Œuvres complètes*, eds. Henri Mondor and G. Jean-Aubry (Paris: Pléiade, 1945), 363–64.
9 Richard Rorty, "Relations, Internal and External," in *The Encyclopedia of Philosophy*, ed. Paul Edwards (New York: Macmillan, 1967), vol. 7, 125–32, interprets this Hegelian figure in directions suggestive for its apotheosis among the *symbolistes*.
10 Villiers de L'Isle-Adam praises Mallarmé for according attention to Hegel, "ce miraculeux génie," in correspondence of September 11, 1866.

sonorité [...]").[11] In a similar vein, in reference to his work of classification as a poetic philologist in "Les mots anglais," Mallarmé writes of "the sense, certainly, and the sound ably tried and tested by one another" ("Le sens, certes, et le son, habilement essayés l'un à l'autre [...]").[12] Something analogous can be said for the visual register of iconic form in its interaction with meaning.

Thus, there is in Mallarmé an aspiration toward the ideality of pure sense, but not as a clean escape from the material world. On the contrary, precisely the role of materiality and mortality in the realization of this sense is what interests him most. The fleetingness and ephemerality of words vanishing into their material effects is what opens their sense beyond its conceptual limits to the ideal—the whole and total. In "Crise de vers," Mallarmé writes of "the pure notion" ("la notion pure") and of an "intellectual word" ("l'intellectuelle parole") and aims at an ideal, transcendental consciousness that can be perfected only in death. Consequently, in *Igitur*, he enacted a literary suicide, extinguishing self-consciousness ("conscience de soi"). It is by means of such a deadly, but also "immortal," word ("immortelle parole") that he endeavors "materially" to find "the truth" in a single stroke ("trouveraient, par une frappe unique, elle-même matériellement la vérité," "Crise de vers," 364). This immortal word is a version of the "essential word" ("parole essentielle") that he contrasts with the "brute word" ("parole brut") a little later in the same essay (368). The latter informs the journalistic "universal *reporting*" ("universel *reportage*") of contemporary writing, to which literature is the shining exception ("la littérature exceptée," 368).

Intrinsic Meanings of Things Expressed through Symbols

In the symbol, the meaning of things themselves, not just of linguistic tokens or semiological cyphers, is made articulate and indeed eloquent. Materially real things such as sounds and graphic marks are placed in intimate, intricate relation with ideal notions or abstract meanings, and the interactions between the two, the fusions created in comprehension, make these concrete materials constitutive of meaning rather than just mechanically instrumental in the signifying process. By this means, signification, rather than consisting in abstract relations of difference in a system of significances, or of mere concepts, becomes material and concrete. In the symbol, linguistic sense becomes poetic sensuousness, to echo the pithy formula of linguist Roman Jakobson. Or, conversely, "Words similar in sound are drawn together in

---

11 Mallarmé, *Œuvres complètes* (1945), 368.
12 Mallarmé, "Les mots anglais," *Œuvres complètes* (1945), 919.

meaning" ("Linguistics and Poetics: Closing Statement," 371). It is not just that sound supplants sense but rather that sound is divulged as intrinsically meaningful in its employment in the symbolist poem, while sense or meaning is made to become sensuous by its incarnation in the poetic word.

Literary theorist Roland Barthes takes this transmogrification of phonic and graphic form into sense, and vice versa, to be the overarching project of modern poetry. The goal is to attain to the sense of things themselves. In Barthes's structuralist linguistic understanding, poetry endeavors "to re-transform the sign into sense: its ideal, tendentially, would be to attain not the sense of words but the sense of things themselves" ("retransformer le signe en sens: son idéal—tendanciel—serait d'atteindre non au sens des mots, mais au sens des choses mêmes").[13]

In somewhat more technical linguistic terms, Barthes writes of "infrasignification" and of a "pre-semiological" state of language. Such instances of language regress to the sort of "natural" signification that is traditionally attributed to the symbol. In this regard, and in the terms of Barthes's semiological theory, poetry contrasts with the totalizing constructions of language that appropriate it in order to signify some superimposed meaning or "myth." For example, the image of a black soldier in uniform saluting the French flag is intended to signify the loyalty of African colonies to a triumphant French imperialism. The natural content of the image is co-opted into a second-order system of signification attributing a meaning to it that is not intrinsic to the image per se, thereby creating a myth. For Barthes, "Contemporary poetry is *a regressive semiological system*. While myth aims at an ultra-signification, an amplification of a primary system, poetry on the contrary attempts to recuperate an infra-signification, a pre-semiological state of language" ("La poésie contemporaine est *un système sémiologique régressif.* Alors que le mythe vise à une ultra-signification, à l'amplification d'un système premier, la poésie au contraire tente de retrouver une infra-signification, un état pré-sémiologique du langage," 241).

Along similar lines, in *La révolution du langage poétique*, Kristeva envisages the most essential type of meaning in poetic language as operating below the level of semantic and syntactic convention. The "pulsions" from which this essential sort of poetic meaning arises are made manifest by deformations of the regular forms and structures of language. The idea that linguistic forms should have intrinsic significances and natural affinities with the things they signify has, as a rule, been rejected in philosophical and linguistic theory at least since Hermogenes's conversation with Cratylus, as recorded or invented

---

13 Roland Barthes, "Le mythe, aujourd'hui," *Mythologies* (Paris: Seuil, 1957), 239, 241.

in Plato's eponymous dialogue, the *Cratylus*. This rejection was upheld by Saint Augustine in his theory of given signs such as verbal sounds and letters (*signa data*) as signifying not by nature but by will and consent ("non natura, sed placito et consensione significandi," *De doctrina christiana* II, xxiv, 37). Linguistic signs taken in themselves were later demoted to mere empty sound or wind, *flatus vocis*, in medieval linguistic theories. The theory of language as conventional finds one of its canonical formulations in the Saussurian principle of the arbitrary character of the linguistic sign. Nevertheless, such natural or material affinities between words and the things they signify are explored intensively in their theoretical reflections on poetry by the *symboliste* poets, as well as being a constitutive principle of their poetic creations.

An especially provocative and influential example of treating language as reified through the concrete properties of its signifiers perceived as things is Rimbaud's attribution of intrinsic meanings to vowel sounds based on their sensuous qualities in "Voyelles": "A noir, E blanc, I rouge, U vert, O bleu, voyelles [...]" ("A black, E white, I red, U green, O blue, vowels [...]"). In the verses that follow this opening line, the specific colors are treated as inherent in each of the vowels and are accordingly drawn out of their "latent births" ("naissances latentes"), connecting the letters directly with a plethora of colored objects and sense impressions of color. Some synaesthetically related sounds also figure, for instance, in the buzzing flies and blaring trumpets. These connections are apparently suggested by analogies between the vowel's timbre and the color-tones of the objects. They may also have been prompted by an illustrated alphabet book (*abécédaire*) for children in common use in France in Rimbaud's time.

VOYELLES

A noir, E blanc, I rouge, U vert, O bleu, voyelles,
Je dirai quelque jour vos naissances latentes.
A, noir corset velu des mouches éclatantes
Qui bombillent autour des puanteurs cruelles,

Golfes d'ombre : E, candeur des vapeurs et des tentes,
Lance des glaciers fiers, rois blancs, frissons d'ombelles ;
I, pourpres, sang craché, rire des lèvres belles
Dans la colère ou les ivresses pénitentes ;

U, cycles, vibrements divins des mers virides,
Paix des pâtis semés d'animaux, paix des rides
Que l'alchimie imprime aux grands fronts studieux

O, suprême Clairon plein de strideurs étranges,
Silences traversés des Mondes et des Anges :
— O l'Oméga, rayon violet de Ses yeux ![14]

VOWELS

Black A, white E, red I, green U, blue O: you vowels,
Some day I'll tell the tale of where your mystery lies:
Black A, a jacket formed of hairy, shiny flies
That buzz among harsh stinks in the abyss's bowels;

White E, the white of kings, of moon-washed fogs and tents,
Of fields of shivering chervil, glaciers' gleaming tips;
Red I, magenta, spat-up blood, the curl of lips
In laughter, hatred, or besotted penitence;

Green U, vibrating waves in viridescent seas,
Or peaceful pastures flecked with beasts—furrows of peace
Imprinted on our brows as if by alchemies;

Blue O, great Trumpet blaring strange and piercing cries
Through Silences where Worlds and Angels pass crosswise;
Omega, O, the violet brilliance of Those Eyes![15]

This sonnet is situated in *Une saison en enfer*, where Rimbaud reflects on how he invented the color of each of the five vowels. He exclaims: "I flattered myself that I was inventing a poetic word accessible to all the senses" ("je me flatai d'inventer un verbe poétique accessible à tous les sens" ("Alchimie du Verbe" in *Saison en enfer*). In effect, Rimbaud treats the poetic word as an object of perception in its own right and an object not only for one sense but for "all." Rimbaud also manages to suggest, by the prolific and unbounded associations he makes with each vowel, that all reality is contained in essence in the letters of the alphabet. Something like this happens to be an age-old teaching of the Kabbalah. The vowels are disclosed as constitutive principles of creation, "divine vibratings" ("vibrements divins"), the first light of Creation. Conversely, the violet ray of "His Eyes" is said to be latent within

---

14 Voyelles, poème d'Arthur Rimbaud - poetica.fr. Accessed December 3, 2025.
15 Translation by George Dance, Talk:Vowels - Wikisource, the free online library. Accessed December 3, 2025.

the clarion O of omega ("O l'Oméga, rayon violet de Ses Yeux !"). All that exists in the Creation seems to be latently present in the letters that stand at the verbal artist's command. He fashions them as a magician wields a magic wand. These latent letters are waiting only for poetic evocation in order to be called into actual being and self-manifestation.

Rimbaud's sonnet became a cult object and bequeathed a kind of founding charter to the "Symbolistes" of the 1880s, a movement which, incidentally, remains arguably the most precise reference for the term "symbolisme" in a strict historical sense.[16] This movement emanated from Belgium and thus from near to Rimbaud's own city of origin, Charleville in the Ardennes of northeastern France. The Belgian symbolists, most importantly Maurice Maeterlinck, author of the symbolist play *Pelléas et Mélisande* (1892), also adopted Baudelaire and Mallarmé as the movement's mighty precursors and tutelary divinities or beacons (*phares*). This symbolist current broadened and developed in its extension beyond francophone to especially Anglo-Saxon territories, following a trajectory reaching from Proust and Valéry to Yeats, Eliot, Joyce, and Gertrude Stein. Such, at least, is the movement's extension as ingeniously reconstructed by Edmund Wilson in *Axel's Castle* (1931).[17]

Early on, Arthur Symons's classic work, *The Symbolist Movement in Literature* (1908), propounded a broad notion of symbolism as a turn-of-the-century aesthetic substitute for religion, which had been in decline throughout the nineteenth century after suffering concerted attacks in the eighteenth century, the Age of Reason. Symons suggested that "in speaking to us so intimately, so solemnly, as only religion had hitherto spoken to us, it [literature] becomes itself a kind of religion, with all the duties and responsibilities of the sacred ritual."[18] This movement was in revolt against the exteriority and superficiality of materialist culture. It was also motivated by a desire for a spiritual renewal in terms less overtly doctrinaire and more aesthetic.

The religious tincture of symbolist aesthetics has continued to be highlighted by numerous critics. Its precedents are treated in extenso in the monumental scholarly synthesis of Paul Bénichou.[19] Standing in this critical lineage, a ground-breaking approach to Mallarmé through religion

---

16 See *La poésie symboliste*, ed. Bernard Delvaille (Paris: Seghers, 1971) and compare Jean Moréas's "Voyelles."

17 Edmund Wilson, *Axel's Castle: A Study in the Imaginative Literature of 1870–1930* (New York: Charles Scribner's Sons, 1959).

18 Arthur Symons, *The Symbolist Movement in Literature* (London: Constable, 1908), 9.

19 Paul Bénichou, *Romantismes français*, 2 vols. (Paris: Gallimard, 2004). Volume I includes *Le sacre de l'écrivain* (1973) and *Le temps des prophètes* (1977). Volume II: *Les mages romantiques* (1988) and *L'école du désenchantement* (1992).

is currently chaperoned by Bertrand Marchal, author of the influential *La religion de Mallarmé*.[20] Mallarmé's "religious" agenda has also evoked strong resonances in many readings by philosophers such as Jacques Rancière, Jean-Claude Milner, and Quentin Meillassoux. In the predominantly literary vein opened by Symons, on the other hand, the reflections of Roberto Calasso prove to be particularly pertinent.[21] In some telling regards, Calasso's cogitations are close to those I have outlined based on the signifying powers peculiar to poetic language, comparing them with powers of theological language.

In Chapter 5 of *La letteratura e gli dèi*, Calasso examines Mallarmé's translation of George W. Cox's *Manuel of Mythology* and observes how Mallarmé systematically changes "God" to "the divinity" ("la divinité"). Calasso writes of an obscure, mysterious bottom or *fond* of all things, from which all spring and originate in Mallarmé's imagining. "God" is a "closed and hidden signifier that inhabits generality" ("significante chiuso e nascosto, che abita la generalità"), and this makes "God" similar to "divinity" ("divinité") as used in Mallarmé's own work (94).

George Cox, as Marchal significantly points out, was an epigone of the German philologist and Orientalist Max Müller (1823–1900).[22] Müller applied the comparative grammar of the Indo-European linguistics developed by Franz Bopp early in the nineteenth century to the study of ancient myths and revolutionized the field by the invention of comparative mythology. In his *Comparative Mythology: An Essay* (*Essay über Vergleichende Mythologie*, 1856), Müller's thesis is that the gods in Indo-European mythology are all born from names and that they become myths by the forgetting of this origin—that is, by the erasure of the original liaison between *numen* (divinity) and *nomen* (name). Müller's reduction of divinity to language was integrated by Mallarmé into his understanding of the world and of life and of poetry's place in them. The myth of divinity is produced simply by *forgetting* its *linguistic* origin and status. We forget that the gods are fiction like everything else within the frame of human culture.

Mallarmé evidently aimed to pursue this theme in his projected *thèse d'agrégation* to be entitled: *De divinitate*. In his writings on religion, Mallarmé postures as revealing the secret kept for two and a half millennia that the gods must be immoral or unseemly in order to be gods. The anthropomorphism of

---

20 Bertrand Marchal, *La religion de Mallarmé: poésie, mythologie et religion* (Paris: J. Corti, 1988). Marchal co-organized with Thierry Roger and Jean-Luc Steinmetz a colloquium on "Spectres de Mallarmé" at CERISY la Salle in July 2019 to which I am indebted for my awareness of recent directions in Mallarmé scholarship. I develop this line of inquiry especially in the companion volume *Mallarmé's Theo-Political Poetics*.
21 Roberto Calasso, *La letteratura e gli dèi* (Milan: Adelphi, 2001).
22 https://www.youtube.com/watch?v=RuDknu6FMoI. Accessed 18/10/2025

Homer's poetically represented divinities had been adduced as an objection against them, as belying their divinity, ever since Xenophon and Plato and again by the Church fathers. Mallarmé, in contrast, turns their all-too-human characteristics and comportment into the very identity of the gods, unmasking them as humanly manufactured idols.

Calasso provocatively reads Mallarmé's poetry as expressing the mystery of the universe through the window of consciousness in a manner parallel to Prajapati (the supreme Creator in the Vedic period) in the Brhadaranyaka Upanishad. In support of this reading, Calasso ventures a comparative religions interpretation of the "Sonnet en x." He expounds Mallarmé's "septuor" as reflecting Prajapati's Spatarsi—the *Orsa Maggiore* or Big Dipper.

Mallarmé was introduced to some fundamentals of Buddhism by his friend Henri Cazalis, to whom he recounts his decisive encounter with Nothing in dramatic epistles (especially those of April 28, 1866 and May 14, 1867). However, he basically refused the empirical methods of the comparative religions approach. He understood himself more in alchemical terms as a hierophant and master. As instrumental as philology may have been to his intellectual development, his poetry is fundamentally about the mystery of consciousness, and this mystery is Hegelian or idealist for him. Although the self could be broken down into its material elements, still consciousness was the mysterious source of all. Matter and existence itself become unsoundable mysteries. They are beholden to the mystery of Mind as a mirror in which all things are reflected.

Reading the religious background standing behind Mallarmé's project is crucial and has slowly come to be recognized as such in the criticism. Behind Bertrand Marchal's disclosures, which have had far-reaching echoes and repercussions, stands the work of Gardner Davies, which already draws on Müller's comparative mythology based on solar religions.[23] Davies focuses on Mallarmé's peculiar use of analogy in order to relate all to all. Mallarmé's great work was to be a hymn of the relations of all with all ("hymne [...] des relations entre tout").[24] For Mallarmé, however, this relation is artificially mediated by language and its totalizing of all as symbolized by the book. For Mallarmé, everything in the world exists in order to end up as a book ("tout, au monde, existe pour aboutir à un livre"). For this vision of unity, "man is charged to see divinely" ("L'homme chargé de voir divinement," "Le livre, Instrument spiritual," 378).

---

23 Gardner Davies, *Mallarmé et le drame solaire : essai d'exégèse raisonné* (Paris: José Corti, 1959).
24 Mallarmé, "Le livre. Instrument spiritual," *Œuvres complètes* (1945), 378.

This pursuit of universal analogy, especially through the artifice of language, becomes thematic, for instance, in Mallarmé's prose piece "The Demon of Analogy" ("Le démon de l'analogie").[25] Language taken as pure sound is a nothingness ("le son *nul*") cut off from the world of facts and things. It nevertheless recoups everything virtually within the emptiness of signification ("le vide de signification"). Language, being itself dead and empty, can be filled artificially and *signify* anything and everything. This makes language "penultimate" to absolute or ultimate reality in that it relates immediately to the absolute or All. It does so simply by what it is concretely as sign (sound or image): it directly incarnates signifying being. Language, by this means, is resurrected as a glorious or ideal body.

Mallarmé's prose texts work out with great intricacy his notion of the vertical metaphoricity of language that opens in its meaning to an infinite, ideal realm yet remains fully embodied and material in its physical existence. As such, language constitutes a glorious body and performs the sacrament of a transfiguration of the real. The real is converted and transposed into the ideal through language, especially by the poet's savant orchestration of sounds and ideas. In his prose portrait of Banville, Mallarmé explains that this "*divine transposition*, for the accomplishment of which man exists, *goes from the fact to the ideal*" ("*La divine transposition*, pour l'accomplissement de quoi existe l'homme, *va du fait à l'idéal*").[26]

The musical vocabulary ("transposing," etc.) is ubiquitous in symbolist poetics. Music, after all, is not just a mechanical production of strings, brass, and wind but the "intellectual word at its apogee, which must, with plenitude and evidence, result from the ensemble of relations existing in the whole" ("l'intellectuelle parole à son apogée que doit avec plénitude et évidence, résulter, en tant que l'ensemble des rapports existant dans tout, la Musique," "Crise de vers," 368). There is a musicality dwelling already within language even before the poet begins to orchestrate its dissonances and harmonies, and this inherent music is the profounder source of the poetry of language. Without setting words to music as an external supplement, the poet elicits from language its inherent musicality.

In "Crise de vers," Mallarmé envisages a fullness of expression that writers should "take back" from music ("reprendre notre bien," 367) and integrate

---

25 "Le démon de l'analogie," *Œuvres complètes* (1945), 272–73. Jean-Michel Rabaté, *La pénultième est morte : Spectrographies de la modernité (Mallarmé, Breton, Beckett et quelques autres)* (Paris: Champs Vallon, 1993) and Eric Benoit, *Le démon de l'analogie, ou : la résurrection des mots* (Bordeaux: Presses Universitaires de Bordeaux, 2022) deeply probe Mallarmé on this issue.

26 Mallarmé, *Œuvres complètes* (1945), 522.

into the total art of the Book ("un art d'achever la transposition, au Livre," 367). This art opens a further dimension beyond that of signifier, signified, and referent, familiar from the Saussurian model. It is what Robert Cohn treats as a fourth pole in a "tetrapolar" scheme.[27] This is the dimension Mallarmé describes in religious terms as a "glorious body," "suave" and "even more ideal" ("plus idéale encore").[28] He designates it also as the higher "virtual" dimension produced by "fiction" and consisting in a virtually sacred art of dream and song ("le dire, avant tout, rêve et chant, retrouve chez le Poëte, par nécessité constitutive d'un art consacré aux fictions, sa virtualité," "Crise de vers," 368). This is the word returned from the brute state to which it is degraded as mere information or "reportage" to its essentiality ("le double état de la parole, brut ou immédiat ici, là essentiel," 368) such that the object evoked "bathes in a new atmosphere." Understanding this essentiality requires anatomizing language into its constitutive elements.

The Pre-semiological and Sub-semantic

Mallarmé is a poet of language, above all, and his innovations demand to be understood in linguistic terms. According to Jakobson's theory, "the poetic function projects the principle of equivalence from the axis of selection onto the axis of combination" ("Linguistics and Poetics: Closing Statement," 358). This means that words are chosen because of equivalences in form or sound with the words preceding or following them in the verbal sequence rather than strictly for how they compare in meaning with other approximately equivalent terms that might be selected instead. Even in the political campaign slogan "I like Ike," the proper name is chosen over other possibilities (like "Eisenhower") because of its similarities in sound with the other words with which it is combined. The forms of language motivate word choice, and meaning results from these forms rather than being simply a function of the objects indicated and referenced.

Linguistic form begins with grammar, and symbolist poetry taps into a pre-semiological level of meaning in language by savant exploitation of grammatical inflections. Roman Jakobson and Claude Levi-Strauss singled out the poetry of Baudelaire as exemplary for illustrating this type of meaning.[29]

---

27 Robert Greer Cohn, *Mallarmé's Divagations: A Guide and Commentary* (New York: Peter Lang, 1990), 251 et passim.

28 In "Ce que disaient les trois cigognes," *Œuvres complètes*, ed. Bertrand Marchal (Paris: Gallimard, 1998), I, 460. Citations of Mallarmé's poetry and prose (excepting his letters) are otherwise from the 1945 Pléiade edition.

29 "'Les Chats' de Charles Baudelaire," *L'Homme*, II, January-April (1962): 5–21. See, further, Jakobson, "Poetry of Grammar and the Grammar of Poetry," *Lingua* XXI (1968): 597–609.

The "poetry of grammar" works by systems of equivalences in grammatical form along the metonymic axis, the axis of "combination," which then *in*form the relations among the meanings projected by the text on its metaphoric axis, the axis of "equivalence." Especially in poetry, setting words alongside each other in syntactic combination has its effect on the meanings for which they are selected according to semantic paradigms. Moreover, patterns and correspondences in grammatical structure are similar to the musical value of verse in inhabiting the manifest form of language anterior to projections of sense. This means that the immediate, explicit forms of locutions prior to their semantic interpretation have properties appreciable in and of themselves. However, for Kristeva, with her theory of "the semiotic" ("le sémiotique"), it is rather the *deformations* of the regular structures of language that manifest a meaning more primitive than the semantic.

The Freudian/Lacanian psychology developed by Kristeva and applied to the study of Mallarmé and Lautréament describes poetic language as motored by "pulsions" or corporeal impulses which are intrinsically intentional: they "veulent dire" or "want to say" something. They may be said, in this sense, to be "psychosomatic." This basic pulsional level of human being is a dynamic, kinetic reality that speaks without resort to the sign and the absence inherent in signs. This level of meaning is sensuously concrete, and its presence in poetry makes poetry into concretely speaking being. By its privileging of the semiotic dynamism of language, therefore, poetry would succeed in achieving a speech which manifests being sensorially. In poetry, language can show forth as speaking being concretely rather than only as always merely indicating the absence of a tangible reality. Except in becoming poetic, language rather represents or faintly images reality from its own condition of exile as separated from things by the break of the sign, its fracture into signifier and signified.

The idea that the signifier should be *per se* significant engenders an atomization of language to its alphabetical components in the search for intrinsic meanings. Speculations on the intrinsic significatory values of letters were carried out by Mallarmé in his poems but also, more explicitly, in his prose writings. Mallarmé's study "Les mots anglais," his most extensive work, as well as his consistent poetic practice, relentlessly stress the meaning inherent within words as sound and icon—or as sensuously perceptible forms apart from their conventional sense. This is the material ground and basis for Mallarmé's "piety" paid to "the twenty-four letters" ("une piété aux vingt-quatre lettres"). These letters are then "transfigured into the "supernatural term," which is the verse" ("jusqu'à une transfiguration en le terme surnaturel, qu'est le vers").[30]

---

30 Mallarmé, "La musique et les lettres," *Œuvres complètes* (1945), 646.

For example, a letter like V in Mallarmé's poems visibly and iconically embodies its meanings rather than merely signifying them arbitrarily by convention. Mallarmé saw images and imitations of the female shape and anatomy in this letter and also in its doubling by the English letter W. Certainly, Vs can be discerned in the ideal figure of the hourglass for the female silhouette. This body shape consists schematically of one V inverted and joined vertically with another at a point corresponding to the waistline. Such an image of femininity was cultivated conspicuously in Victorian times, with which Mallarmé's lifetime coincided. Both *v* and *w* were thus naturally suited to evoke aspects of femininity in words like *V*enus, *v*ierge, *v*agina, and *w*oman.

This is one example in a visual register of how the letter can signify iconically and concretely already in itself as a physical shape and form independently of its employment as a component part in a word. Accordingly, the materially present signifier becomes a concrete embodiment of meaning, an icon or even an idol. Just such a use of this letter as visible verbal icon is made conspicuous in Mallarmé's sonnet "Le *v*ierge, le *v*ivace et le bel aujourd'hui." This letter is used iconically also in "Hérodiade," with its focus on the cult of *v*irginity. Words including *victime*, *vigie*, *volets*, *vitres*, *vitrage*, *vitrail*, *vols*, *vélin* discretely carry this connotation, which becomes conspicuous in a line like: "Le *v*ieil éclat *v*oilé du *v*ermeil insolite, / De la *v*oix languissante" ("The *v*enerable *v*eiled brightness of the exotic *v*ermilion / of the languishing *v*oice").

Alongside visual iconography, the aesthetics of music also accord with this privileging of the sub-semantic and pre-semiological levels of meaning as the most crucially significant in symbolist art. "De la musique avant toute chose" ("Music before all other things") wrote Verlaine in his "Ars poétique" at the head of his prescriptions for the art of (symbolist) poetry. Music had already been exploited by Romantics like Richard Wagner for its inimitable capacity to express the irrational. Finding no other outlet, given the general demise of religion in modern times, these trans-rational or supra-rational impulses motivated the new wave of poetry that, according to Marcel Raymond, flowed from Baudelaire to Surrealism.[31]

Music, as a non-representational art, features the immediate emotional value of sounds that are significant without being co-opted into a semiological system. Thus, *symboliste* language can readily be understood as a kind of music which signifies immediately on the basis of the sensibly audible qualities of its verbal signifiers rendered resonant and significant independently of the conventional determinations by the semantic meanings of those sounds combined into words. Of course, this is only a relative independence. Even if the conceptual sense is not fixed and static, it typically plays into the

---

31 Marcel Raymond, *De Baudelaire au surréalisme* (Paris: Librairie José Corti, 1963).

vibration of the word as it oscillates between sense and sonority, as revealed by Mallarmé in "Crise de vers" (368) and as elaborated by Paul Valéry. In his "Commentaire de 'Charmes'," Valéry stresses that poetry's rhythms and sonorities engage "the entire sentient being" ("tout l'être sentant"). He plays up the physicality of words, "their effects of induction or their mutual influences, which dominate at the expense of their property of being consumed in definite and certain sense" ("rapprochments physiques de mots, leurs effets d'induction ou leurs influences mutuelles qui dominant, aux dépens de leur propriétié de se consommer en un sens défini et certain").[32]

Mallarmé takes this type of reflection on music especially to the level of the letter. In "La musique et les lettres," he sees writing as an "arabesque" that forms a type of musical composition (648). Verse is, in itself, a musical form. In this essay (originally a lecture delivered in Oxford and Cambridge), Mallarmé emphasizes the omnipresence of verse wherever there is any kind of rhythm or stylistic effort in writing. Since there is then no prose, there is no poetry either (the two terms are correlative), but simply rhythms in language making manifest the expression of style, and this is "literature." In "Crise de vers," Mallarmé had written that "the form called verse is simply literature itself" ("la forme appelée vers est simplement elle-même la littérature," 361). Literature has evaded all the canons of rhetoric and can be created by any individual's own idiosyncratic rhythm, which however should correspond to an obscure substrate or "fond" in us all, a "ground" from which all things come, according to the order of universal symbolism. The poet is no longer the voice of a community. He has exited, and has even been exiled from, society. Nevertheless, he still interprets some kind of universal "Orphic" nature.

At this point, it might well be asked why the symbolists should bother with language at all. Why not just elicit universal meaning immediately from pure sound and shape and color? Indeed, music and painting count as eminent art forms of the Symbolist movement. The account given so far seems to make almost irrelevant the fact that the sounds and forms in question, as infinitely productive of meaning, are language and belong to words. But this would be to ignore what Mallarmé calls "the mystery in letters" ("Le mystère dans les lettres," *Œuvres complètes* [1945], 382–87)—the mysterious fact that these bits of matter that make up letters *signify*. And they are perhaps only the most outspoken heralds of a much more general predicament.

There is often an at least implicit theory, assumed when not consciously articulated by symbolist writers, that the essence of the thing is speech, or in other words, that being is intrinsically speaking. The sound, the color, accordingly, are not understood until we understand what they *say*.

---

32 Valéry, *Variété* III (Paris: Gallimard, 1936), 79.

This amounts to making the whole universe an allegory for intelligent, linguistic activity. Being itself is read as an allegory for speaking. This may be the speech of Nature, as for a Romantic (like Nerval, in "Vers dorés": "'Tout est sensible !' [...] À la matière même un verbe est attaché ..."), or of God in his Creation by the Word or *Verbum*, as for Dante. Or it may be received simply as the voice of the absolute Void, as for Mallarmé. Thus, the poetic word can be privileged above all other beings because it most immediately reveals the essence of being itself as a kind of speaking. The being which underlies the sign as signifier, that is, the materiality of the signifier, is itself speaking being.

The symbolists' fixation on the word itself and its component parts as each in itself a plenum of being is predicated on, and motivated by, a perhaps sometimes latent, subliminal view that being per se is speech. At least this is the ultimate implication of symbolist aesthetics. Even though natural beings are more immediately the speech of being than is human language, where absence and non-being come into play as constitutive principles of signification, nevertheless the analogy of words to being *qua* speech is closer than that of material objects. Words are transparently—while material objects are opaquely—speaking being. Consequently, human speech, after all, is the most apt of all types of things to reveal being in its inherent nature as speaking.

The *symbolistes* recovered this pre-modern symbolic worldview in various ways, perhaps most explicitly and emblematically in Baudelaire's "Correspondances," where Nature, with its living trees or "pillars," is a temple from which issue enigmatic words ("La Nature est un temple où de vivants piliers / Laissent parfois sortir de confuses paroles"), but with a difference. The *symbolistes*, by and large, and certainly Mallarmé, were secular spirits, and their vision of the world as consisting in mysterious correspondences was now considered to be the product not of God or of Nature, but of artifice. The *symbolistes* belonged to an age of discovery of the religion of art. This can be shown in relation to various authors (Huysmans, Gide, etc.), but it can be demonstrated with particular penetration in relation to Mallarmé, largely because of the latter's lifelong speculations, which have come more and more to light, about how poetry repurposes and repackages religion.[33]

There is, of course, a well-known theological tradition based on this view that being is itself in some sense speech, or at least originates in speech, namely, the Logos, the Word, as Creator. As proclaimed in the Gospel According to John: "All things were made by him [the Word, ὁ λόγος]; and without him was not anything made that was made" (John 1: 3). The decline of this doctrine

---

33 In addition to Bertrand Marchal, *La religion de Mallarmé : poésie, mythologie et religion*, see Marchal and Jean-Luc Steinmetz, eds., *Mallarmé ou l'obscurité lumineuse* (Paris: Hermann, 1999).

besieged by myriad materialisms in modern times may well be an important motivation for the rise of a Romantic-Symbolist metaphysics, as Marcel Raymond suggested. Once the worldview implied in Christian theology was felt to be no longer viable, new interpretations of speaking being needed to be found, and symbolist poetry found some of the most compelling of them. Baudelaire, in particular, occupies an emblematic place in the matrix of this symbolist vision of things as language and of language as a sort of quasi-natural thing.[34] The symbolist current following him can thus be seen to emerge as a radicalization of Romanticism.[35] The reflections I advance in this book pursue the profound and disturbing ambiguities of this symbolic vision as it was handed down from Baudelaire to his heirs.

In pre-modern poetry, the ideal of the poet was often said to be to learn to hear the native language of things. Even Baudelaire, in "L'invitation au voyage," puts it this way in saying that in the place of his desire, all things will speak secretly to his soul "its sweet native language" ("Tout y parlerait / A l'âme en secret / Sa douce langue natale"). He expresses a similar intuition again in "Élévation," evoking "the language of flowers and mute things" ("Le langage des fleurs et des choses muettes"). But the symbolist aesthetic developed by Mallarmé is acutely aware that things do not of their own nature speak. In the positivistic scientific worldview of the nineteenth century, things are dead, dumb matter and nothing else in and of themselves. They can be *made* to speak only by the imaginative ingenuity of human subjects. Particularly poets. This is the vocation of poetry—to make something to be experienced not simply as it is, but as humans might wish and dream it to be. Mallarmé's "Crise de vers" exposes this predicament baldly and explicitly as producing "fiction."[36]

---

34 I have elsewhere examined more closely Baudelaire's work in mediating the Romantic notion of symbolic language to French symbolist poetry based on viewing the word as a thing in "The Linguistic Turning of the Symbol: Baudelaire and his French Symbolist Heirs," Chapter 6 of *Secular Scriptures: Modern Theological Poetics in the Wake of Dante* (Columbus: Ohio State University Press, 2016), 143–68. An earlier version of the essay appeared in *Baudelaire and the Poetics of Modernity*, volume in Honor of Claude Pichois, ed. Patricia Ward (Nashville: Vanderbilt University Press, 2000), 28–40.

35 On French Romantic poets as supernaturalists and "magicians," see Paul Bénichou, *Les mages romantiques* (Paris: Gallimard, 1988). Bénichou's *Selon Mallarmé* (Paris: Gallimard, 1995), 11–71, traces the path from the Romantics to Mallarmé.

36 "Crise de vers," 368. Cf. also "Notes," of 1869, where every method is dubbed a "fiction." Fiction is deemed the very process of the human spirit and of self-reflection in language ("Toute méthode est une fiction [...]. Le langage se réfléchissant. Enfin la fiction lui semble être le procédé même de l'esprit humain," *Œuvres complètes* [1945], 851).

Mallarmé was all too aware that sense and natural form sometimes, and even generally, fail to completely correspond in a given word due to contingencies ("le hasard") inherent in linguistic history. They may even be contradictory to each other, as in the case of the heavy sound of the word *jour* for "day" and the acute sound of the word *nuit* for "night" in spite of the fact that the "things" so named are just the opposite according to their natural qualities. The day, with its bright light, has a piercing sharpness opposite to the night's heavy obscurity and bluntness. But that paradox, in Mallarmé's view, is precisely where the skill of the writer comes in to make the effect of *jour* exalted and celestial, even though in French the word sounds "heavy" and earthbound.

As Mallarmé explains in "Crise de vers," words often do not sound at all like the things they name. He finds it disappointing that the word "ténèbres" (*darkness*) is not deep or opaque in sound, but rather light, just as the timbre of "nuit" ("night") is much brighter than that of "jour" ("day"). He writes, "Alongside *ombres* (*shadow*), which is opaque, *ténèbres* (*darkness*) is not very deep; what a disappointment in face of the perversity conferring on *day* (*jour*) as on *night* (*nuit*) contradictorily timbres that in the first case are obscure and in the second clear." ("A côté d'*ombre*, opaque, *ténèbres* se fonce peu ; quelle déception, devant la perversité conférant à *jour* comme à *nuit*, contradictoirement, des timbres obscurs ici, là clair," 364). Mallarmé concludes, however, that verse can make up for this defect by supplying philosophically, as a kind of "superior complement," what "languages lack" ("[...] le vers: lui, philosophiquement rémunère le défaut des langues, complément supérieur," 364).

Thus, Mallarmé concedes that ordinary language is purely arbitrary in assigning sounds to things, but he counts on poetry to artificially create correspondences that seem natural to us. The art of poetry can make the pure arbitrariness of language seem motivated. The analogies between the sounds of words and the natural qualities of things are just accidental, but they can be exploited by art to create analogies in what constitutes a kind of "secondary Cratylism."[37] An artificially devised fittingness can be superimposed and create a certain illusion of language's natural meaningfulness, even though this disguises or dissembles its deeper arbitrariness and indeterminacy. More than these principles themselves, the poems Mallarmé creates by means of them manifest something rather miraculous in its effects. Art striving to overcome chance remains the theme of Mallarmé's final, definitive work, the *Coup de dés*.

---

37 Illuminating on this topic is Judy Kravis, *The Prose of Mallarmé: The Evolution of a Literary Language* (Cambridge: Cambridge University Press, 1976), 76, 81.

Chapter 2

ILLUSTRATIVE READINGS OF MALLARMÉ'S POEMS AS SYMBOLIST WORKS

We will be able to visit just a few intensely instructive examples of Mallarmé's poetry, focusing especially on his "meta-poetry," or on how his writing exposes the poetic process as it realizes our human predicament of being in language. Leading the troop, the "Sonnet en x" stages an allegory of the signifying process enacted by poetic language as a drama of to be *as* not to be. It invites, even more conspicuously than most other poems by Mallarmé, a penetrating regard into the workings of his negative poetics. The ambiguity of language, its positive presence yet emptiness of the reality it represents, as foregrounded in this poem, opens to view a virtual ontological dimension of human existence that all too easily passes unperceived. This sonnet, with its compact virtuoso performance of the theoretical premises of Mallarmean poetics, illustrates exemplarily his unprecedented reinvention of the symbol.

In this famous "Sonnet en x" ("Ses purs ongles"), the key letter x figuratively depicts, by its form as a letter, the coordinated axes of sense and sonority on which the poem is erected and suspended. Moreover, rotating the X by 45 degrees fits these axes to a Crucifixion motif: ✝. In his letter to Henri Cazalis of July 18, 1868, Mallarmé tellingly avows concerning this sonnet that "the sense, if there is one ...... is evoked by an internal mirage of the words themselves" ("le sens, s'il en a un ...... est évoqué par un mirage interne des mots mêmes").[1] This does not mean that their referential sense counts for nothing but rather that it counts only as negated so that the "sense" is projected internally from the words themselves as sounds and shapes. Indeed, the sounds should be heard as echoing in a consciousness tense with some of the most pregnant senses conceivable. In this specific case, a sense as momentous as the death of God on the cross, the crucified Word, can be inferred in numerous ways from the hermetic images.

---

[1] *Œuvres complètes* (1998), I, 731.

Sonnet en x ("Ses Purs Ongles")

Ses purs ongles très haut dédiant leur onyx,
L'Angoisse, ce minuit, soutient, lampadophore,
Maint rêve vespéral brûlé par le Phénix
Que ne recueille pas de cinéraire amphore

Sur les crédences, au salon vide : nul ptyx,
Aboli bibelot d'inanité sonore
(Car le Maître est allé puiser des pleurs au Styx
Avec ce seul objet dont le Néant s'honore.)

Mais proche la croisée au nord vacante, un or
Agonise selon peut-être le décor
Des licornes ruant du feu contre une nixe,

Elle, défunte nue en le miroir, encore
Que, dans l'oubli fermé par le cadre, se fixe
De scintillations sitôt le septuor.[2]

Sonnet in x ("Its pure nails")

Its pure nails on high dedicating their onyx,
Anguish this midnight upholds like a torch
Many vesperal dreams burned by the Phoenix
Gathered by no urn in any cinerary porch

On the console, in the empty room: no ptyx
Abolished bibelot of sonorous inanity
(For the Master left to draw tears from the Styx
With this object claimed by the void's vanity).

But near the vacant northern casement, an ore
Agonizes perhaps according to the décor
Of unicorns pursuing a nymph in a rix,

She, like a cloud in the mirror, an encore
In which the frame's empty stage can fix
Presto! The glittering stars of the septuor.[3]

---

2 Mallarmé's poems are cited here and throughout from *Œuvres complètes* (1945).
3 Mallarmé, *Sonnets*, trans. David Scott (Exeter: Shearsman Books, 2008), 85.

In "Ses purs ongles" (the "Sonnet en x"), signification comes across as a voiding of meaning referenced to an external world, a movement toward the emptiness of signs that remain purely as traces, gestures of sonority anchored to no determinate meaning extrinsic to themselves. These signifiers must, rather, be motivated internally to the poem. Absolute meaning is thereby concentrated into the poem's own verbal structure. Such language in its empty sonority emerges as "the Nothing that honors itself" ("le Néant s'honore"). A scintillating constellation of sound patterns is what remains once meaning has been evacuated—or rather has become purely immediate, identical with its signifiers, which remain mysteriously surcharged with indeterminate meaning in their vibrating aura. Substituting themselves for any exterior referent, they have the ambiguous, not to say uncanny, quality of making the world disappear while they remain as its simulacrum, projecting a meaning beyond matter in a world of pure virtuality.

Mallarmé's sonnet evacuates language to the limit of its ability to make statements of a subject–object nature with logical syntax. At the same time, it surcharges language with meaning, managing to suggest a whole scenario freighted with a surplus of significance. What happens when language, by *hollow*ing out semantic significance, becomes a *hallow*ing of nothingness? For Maurice Blanchot, in *L'espace littéraire*, the "central point" is where "the accomplishment of language coincides with its disappearance" ("l'accomplissement du langage coïncide avec sa disparition"), where everything is spoken, where "all is word, but where the word is no longer itself anything but the appearance of that which has disappeared, is the imaginary, the incessant, and the interminable" ("tout est parole, mais où la parole n'est plus elle-même que l'apparence de ce qui a disparu, est l'imaginaire, l'incessant et l'interminable," 45, 46).

The sonnet has been cogently read as an enactment of the death of God.[4] The Phoenix, or the daily-dying-and-rising-again sun, burns "many evening dreams" ("maint rêves vespéral")—alluding to human hopes and dreams and to the evening liturgical office of Vespers. This phoenix's ashes are gathered by *no* amphora. The daily death of the god results in an emptiness monumentalized by the *absence* of material remains in a linguistic structure designed for conserving the memory of death. Dreams, after all, are meaning "burned" by daylight or full consciousness, but they can be conserved in some sort by midnight anxiety—even if only in being dispersed. Ellen Burt, reading the poem as about the undoing of meaning as intentional expression, suggests that "The inner, subjective 'content' is not

---

4 Alfred G. Engstrom, "Mallarmé and the Death of God: The 'sonnet en—x,'" *Romance Notes* 22/3 (1982): 302–307.

grasped, not 'collected' in these images."⁵ Instead, the images are dispersed and emptied of meaning. Such is their peculiarly negative way of meaning: it releases meaning into its infinity and propels it to indeterminacy. All this reads inversely as an intensification of meaning to the zero degree.

The anxiety at midnight of the first two verses is sustained by the moon as bearer of light, literally (or etymologically) "lampadophore." This emotion itself takes over from linguistic signification in spreading the awareness engendered by the poem crystalized in its pure nails "dedicating" their hard mineral surface, their "onyx," on high ("Se purs ongles très haut dédiant leur onyx"). The metaphorically mentioned stellar constellations, literally fingernails, evoke nervous—even praying—fingers that are a parodic figure pointing to the highly exalted ("très haut") divinity. The shiny "nails" are visible like the stars of the sky at night and yet are truly felt in their transcendence above everything worldly only as anguish inwardly, their emotional correlative. Precisely this inwardness is being emptied out since language is apotheosized into an absolute state by this poem. Anguish is metamorphosed into an objective constellation of words mirroring the cosmic constellations.

Everything mentioned is in some way negated. Like no amphora, so also "no ptyx" ("nul ptyx") is evoked as *not* standing on the "credences," which ambiguously connote religious beliefs (*credo, credere*), as well as pieces of furniture (sideboards or buffets) in an "empty salon" ("salon vide"). This "ptyx" may be conceived of as a seashell re-sounding with echoes of emptiness (making the ocean sound again when it is absent), or equally as a *writing* tablet, a fold, a receptacle (Burt 99). There is actually no such word in French. It is more plausibly Greek. Or one could think also of the English *pyx*, the name of a container for the Eucharist used to carry communion to the sick or disabled.

But according to Mallarmé's own commentary in his letter of May 3, 1868 to Lefébure, "ptyx" may not exist in any language ("mot *ptyx* [...] n'existe dans aucune langue," 728–29). As Mallarmé's own creation by the magic of rhyme ("afin de me donner le charme de le créer par la magie de la rime"), the word stands as just a sound without any standard, shared, or legitimate sense. Without meaning anything that can be referenced in the world, it means nothing more than itself—despite the penumbra of suggestions it bears, none of which however turns out to be verifiable. In effect, it is a trace, a meaningless signifier that voids language of meaning. For Burt, "the ptyx reflects nothing more than itself," "pure tautology," because it is an image of

---

5 Ellen S. Burt, "Mallarmé's 'Sonnet en yx': The Ambiguities of Speculation," in Harold Bloom, ed., *Stéphane Mallarmé* (New York: Chelsea, 1987), 105.

no thing yet a residue or trace, a meaningless signifier: a resounding absence because without correspondence to any object as referent. It is, in the words of the poem, a "sonorous inanity" ("inanité sonore"). It is composed of phonetic stops—unpronounceably juxtaposed consonants: p, t, x—in order to gather and hold tear water from the river Styx ("puiser des pleurs au Styx").

Plato's *Cratylus* depicts words rather as flow, *rhea*. They can convey meaning through relations running from word to word in the sequence of the sentence, and there must also be a flow or exchange between words and things. But in Mallarmé's sonnet, representational meaning referring to things is present only to be stopped and voided. This is language that is more like music composed of meaningless, non-referential sounds. The process of evacuation of meaning, of neutering the traces of reference all through the poem, gives it its provocatively suggestive inanity ("inanité sonore"). It is because all things, starting from the highest, the stars in heaven, are ambiguously signified in it that the poem's ultimate evacuation of significance turns out to be so inexhaustibly plenitudinous and telling.

Evelyn Dueck aptly states the poem's "thesis" or revelation concerning repetition and absence in language: "First, written language is a physically present object whose mediality is based on the absence of its referents. This fundamental absence is, second, a condition *sine qua non* of its fictional freedom. Language allows giving a presence to and thus resurrecting things," including things like unicorns and nymphs that do not "really" exist.[6] Self-negating expressions such as "aboli bibelot" ("abolished bagatelle"), "nul ptyx" ("no ptyx"), and "inanitié sonore" ("sonorous inanity") designate unique and curious forms of the existence of nothingness, which then storms riotously onto the scene in these fictional figures suggesting how nothingness can be more boisterously real than what we ordinarily take to be reality.

Dueck discerns in Mallarmé's sonnet a process of "allegorical self-reflexivity" (137–39). Mallarmé's original version of this sonnet sent in a letter to Cazalis (July 18, 1868) was entitled "Sonnet Allegorical of Itself" ("Sonnet allégorique de lui-même," *Œuvres complètes*, I, 1998, 730–33). Dueck's interpretation is that this title had to be erased since the allegory and its self-reflective implications could be realized only through the process of reading and could not be taken as completed from the outset by the printed text itself (139). A subjective dimension of reception necessarily underwrites the reality of nothingness made present by the poem.

---

6 Evelyn Dueck, "Mallarmé's Rhetoric: Allegorical Self-Reflexivity in Mallarmé's Sonnet en –x," in *Self-Reflection in Literature,* eds. Florian Lippert and Marcel Schmid (Leiden: Brill/Rodopi, 2020), 128–41. Citation, 132.

The unique object of the ptyx is absent evidently because the Master has taken it with him in order to draw tears from the classical river of death, the Styx. The Master or the Subject is himself (or itself) absent, and this "object," the ptyx, is nothing but a sonority by which the Nothing is honored—"*s'honore*"—if we hear in this reflexive verb the homophonous "sonore." A sonorous Nothing is certainly what this poem contrives to honor in the highest degree ("très haut"), ironically beginning with a not particularly noble object, a part of the body: fingernails or even toenails ("ongles"), viewed, however, ambiguously as stars and as composed of precious stone ("onyx"). Every item of the universe, presumably, is tinnily sonorous yet also honorific, or possessed of some worth, if it exists in communication with others in forming a great constellation. At the same time, all such components are also teetering on the chasm of annihilation, for their existence together, as purely relational, is evoked and sustained by nothing more than the sonorous words of a sonnet.

The "ptyx" is also simply the word itself as self-emptying—without regard to its meaning, since it has none. This makes it especially suited to be the only object ("seul objet") or instrument that the Master has taken with him to the river of death, the Styx in the underworld, in order to draw tears and then presumably void them of inner intention so that they can be purified of this somber significance and become, in effect, prayers paying homage to Nothing ("ce seul objet dont le Néant s'honore").

Mallarmé's poetry seems to illustrate particularly well how all representational meaning (starting from "God," as representing the Ground of all beings) can be voided, leaving only inane sonority as a trace, a meaning that has been evacuated, a signifier become meaningless.[7] Such poetry becomes a signifier that is without a signified by which it is defined. When the signified is not itself grounded as ontologically distinct from signifiers but rather itself consists in purely differential relations (as in the Saussurian model)—or in other words, when it is neither a self-subsistent thing nor a mental content of meaning—then meaning is constantly emptied out and turned into "inane sonority."

Mallarmé dwells upon the nullity at the heart of language and at the core of meaning in his "Sonnet en x" because that is the dark source of all possible meaning. That phrase, "inanité sonore," which I take to be Mallarmé's description of the essential word and his characterization of universal, original linguistic meaning, applies eminently to the word (if it is a word) "ptyx" in the second quatrain: "nul ptyx, / Aboli bibelot d'inanité sonore." The negation

---

[7] This void, as the departure point for paradoxically robust poetic creation, is analyzed by Eric Benoit in *Néant sonore: Mallarmé ou la traversée des paradoxes* (Geneva: Droz, 2007), 9–13.

("nul ptyx") indicates that this phrase is about a ptyx that is absent. But it may be that this absence is due not only to the Master's having taken with him an object, presumably a shell or a fold, or perhaps a receptacle or writing tablet, to draw tears from the Styx, the river of death. The absence may also obtain because a ptyx is nothing and "ptyx" means nothing.

Nevertheless ("Mais"), as the sextet shows, all correspondence with an external world is not *simply* erased. Near the vacant northern window ("proche la croisée au nord vacante"), a trace of agonizing remains on the "gold" frame ("un or / Agonise") serving as a mirror reflecting "perhaps" a decoration ("selon peut-être le décor"), presumably a picture, perhaps a painting. A window stands as an empty space in the wall, and yet its frame still reflects an anguish which exists in an interior space of a room—but also, and more essentially, in self-reflective self-consciousness.

The mirror reflects, paradoxically, a picture not of emptiness but of ardent erotic desire and sexual violence against a "nixe" ("Des licornes ruant de feu contre une nixe"), presumably a species of nymph, giving dramatic substance on the ground to the burning lights of heaven previously glimpsed above. Strikingly, the violence is perpetrated by unicorns ("licornes"), traditionally chivalric guardians of the chastity of virgins, in another gesture of voiding first-degree meaning by contradiction in order to open toward indeterminate, unconfined meaning by negation. In logical terms, "A" means just one thing whereas "not-A" can mean almost anything—indeed, everything that is not simply "A."

The primordial, perennial drama of sex and violence is closed in a frame of forgetfulness and yet fixed ("Que dans l'oubli fermé par le cadre se fixe"): in language, it is arrested and retained but also forgotten or made absent. Vesperal rays of the setting sun evoke, furthermore, the cosmic drama of the daily dying (and phoenix-like rising again) of the sun god. The window designated, according to its type, with the term "croisée" ("cross-window" divided into four panes by vertical and horizontal mullions crossing at right angles) is not without some reminiscence of the founding self-sacrifice of Christ on the Cross (*croix*) that primal sun cults were taken to prefigure by studies in comparative religions. All this is presented as a trace of a spark from the heavens, a direct reflection of the seven golden stars of the Big Dipper ("De scintillations sitôt le septuor").

The "nixe" is defunct and naked in the reflection ("Elle défunte et nue dans le mirroir"). And yet ("encore que"), while this picture enclosed in its frame and framed again as a reflection in the window would be effectively condemned to oblivion ("dans l'oubli fermé par le cadre"), something else actually happens. Meaning that is fixed through enframing is, in effect, dead and forgotten—no longer connected with living experience. This represented content is cut off from direct relation with anything outside, yet it is also *in itself* a reflection of the cosmos outside. Not by the mediation of any representation, it fixes ("se fixe"), instead, immediately ("sitôt") the scintillations of the cosmos emblematized in the Big Dipper ("le septuor") named in a way resonating with the Pléiades and other poetic constellations. Mallarmé thus reaches in his poetic practice toward an immediacy subverting signification. This would be the divine state of the gods that we will see imagined also by the faun in "L'après-midi d'un faune."

In the "Sonnet en x," Mallarmé manages to make a bourgeois interior, comprising some of the commonplace domestic baubles and banalities of his time, the stage for a cosmic metaphysical drama. The self-enclosed interior works well as a way of depicting the space of self-reflective, "Cartesian" self-consciousness. The "salon," with its sideboards or "credences," becomes the empty space in which otherworldly credos are voided or turned into meaningless material objects, while the Bible, as "bibelot," becomes a bagatelle.

Alluding to the world outside, a racy painting with the mythological motif of unicorns rushing upon a naked nymph hangs near the window at the empty north and shines with agonizing gold tints. However, even beyond and before such allusiveness, the poem reflects on itself—its content on its structure. The *septuor* or seven-star constellation of the end-word alludes to the 4 + 3 formula of quatrains and a sextet consisting of twice three lines that make up the sonnet. The numerical figure of 7 is doubled also in the fourteen lines (= 2 × 7) of the sonnet, just as the scene of forgetting enclosed in a frame ("l'oubli fermé par le cadre") is doubled as reflected in the mirror.[8]

These are all ways in which the sonnet signifies itself and is truly a "Sonnet allégorique de lui-même," as the title of the original version of 1868 explicitly said. Yet the poem, being allegorical, even in signifying itself manages also glancingly to allude to high heaven and the universe, as well as to a typological scene depicted in an interior as refracted within it. The sunset's evidencing a "Crime" consisting in killing God and bloodying the horizon is more explicit in the earlier version of the first stanza. The poem becomes a vehicle of signifying universal analogy by means of deflecting signification to itself. The poem itself emerges as origin and creator of the universe of sense that is accessible to human experience.

X is a letter that stands for crossing out, and this is essential to the operation of the word in evacuating the world of things in order to establish rather the order of the "essential word" ("parole essentielle"), which this sonnet realizes

---

8 D. A. Reynolds, "Illustration, present or absent: Reflecting reflexivity in Mallarmé's 'Sonnet en yx'," *Journal of European Studies* XIX (1989): 311–29.

exemplarily. Mallarmé describes this sonnet as "nil and self-reflecting in every way" ("nul et se réfléchissant de toutes les façons") in his Letter to Cazalis on July 18, 1868 (*Œuvres complètes*, 1998, I, 392-93). It uses sound similarity between locutions to suggest also corresponding meaning that, however, vanishes like a mirage if the reader comes too close (Dueck, 136).

In the "Sonnet en x," the phoneme yx [iks] is the key to rhymes throughout the quatrains and sextet and to the weave of their meaning. The X configures the creation of meaning out of ambiguity. The two axes of the Greek letter *chi* (X) open up a difference within the signifying system itself, without regard to any reality outside it. The arms of the X (or cross) open infinitely on diverging trajectories. The composition thus questions: Could ambiguity be seen as an opening and diverging of the two axes (signified and signifier) from which meaning originates as original difference? Does this not make the symbol, in its own essence, allegorical? The symbol undertakes to erase this difference at its origin, substituting "a tenebrous and profound unity" ("une ténébreuse et profonde unité") in Baudelaire's haunting phrase in "Les Correspondances," and yet it annihilates the difference between language and the real precisely by opening up difference *within* language. The original act of Creation constituted by separation (of heaven from earth and of the waters above the firmament from those below, Genesis 1.1) is echoed in the differential constitution of language itself. Language, thereby, behind its own back, mirrors the real imagined as itself a differential production. Reality is mirrored in the word as constructed on internal differentiation between its axes of signifier and signified. This amphiboly becomes intensely self-conscious in the poetic mirrorings created by Mallarmé's poems.

"Une dentelle s'abolit" offers another mesmerizing example of this magical creation out of nothing through institution of difference in and by the word. The word is essentially a play of difference that analogizes with music as differentiated tones that produce meaning without referring to anything outside themselves. In "Une dentelle s'abolit," the play ("Jeu") produced by a fluttering lace curtain reveals the "eternal absence" of a bed on which birth is given to the poet in the hollow of musical nothing ("au creux néant musicienne"). He is a sort of "musician of silence," in the terms recouped from "Sainte."

The "Sonnet en x," first written in 1868 and published in 1887, stands as an early concentrate and a blueprint for the poetics of Mallarmé's definitive "grand oeuvre," his *Coup de dés*.[9] But the "Sonnet en x" pairs well also with the "Sonnet en i" in its exploration of the incomparable power of the negative that

---

9 It is so read by Annette de la Motte, *Au-delà du mot : Une "écriture du Silence" dans la littérature française au vingtième siècle* (Münster: LIT, 2004), 65-67.

operates in and through language. The latter poem—"Le vierge, le vivace, et le bel aujourd'hui"—provocatively brings out some different aspects of this same power of linguistic negativity. Both poems read perfectly as allegories of writing as understood in Mallarmé's radical symbolist aesthetic based on a coincidence of the opposite extremes of impasse and transcendence. Such is the double lot of anything linguistic exposed through symbolist poetry in all its ambiguity.

Sonnet en i ("Le vierge, le vivace, et le bel aujourd'hui")

"Le vierge, le vivace, et le bel aujourd'hui" (1885), a kind of companion piece to "Ses purs ongles" in the series of sonnets "Plusieurs sonnets," is commonly known as the "Sonnet en i" by virtue of the acute vowel sound "i" at the end of every line. This makes every line point up, so to speak, with a sharp, clear, bright flash. This vector evidently imitates the struggle of the swan to liberate itself from the ice in which it is frozen and trapped and to fly away with one of the "flights that have not fled" ("vols qui n'ont pas fui"). Nevertheless, this mimetic character of the poem's phonetic pattern should be seen not merely as a sensible incarnation of its meaning, or as imitating its sense only at the level of sound, but rather as putting the sense into play also at an intellectual level. This sense is not to be conceived of as a discrete, isolable concept or sensory image but rather as a spiritual value working together in relation to other types of value, including sound, in a thwarted quest to achieve transcendence of the material world.

Sonnet en i

Le vierge, le vivace et le bel aujourd'hui
Va-t-il nous déchirer avec un coup d'aile ivre
Ce lac dur oublié que hante sous le givre
Le transparent glacier des vols qui n'ont pas fui !

Un cygne d'autrefois se souvient que c'est lui
Magnifique mais qui sans espoir se délivre
Pour n'avoir pas chanté la région où vivre
Quand du stérile hiver a resplendi l'ennui.

Tout son col secouera cette blanche agonie
Par l'espace infligée à l'oiseau qui le nie,
Mais non l'horreur du sol où le plumage est pris.

Fantôme qu'à ce lieu son pur éclat assigne,
Il s'immobilise au songe froid de mépris
Que vêt parmi l'exil inutile le Cygne.

    Sonnet in i

The virginal, living and lovely day
Will it fracture for us with a wild wing-blow
This solid lost lake whose frost's haunted below
By the glacier, transparent with flights not made?

A swan from time past remembers it's he
Magnificent yet struggling hopelessly
Through not having sung a liveable country
From the radiant boredom of winter's sterility.

His neck will shake off this whitest agony
Space inflicts on a bird that denies it wholly,
But not earth's horror that entraps his feathers.

Phantom assigned to this place by his brilliance,
The Swan in his exile is rendered motionless,
Swathed uselessly by his cold dream of defiance.[10]

The "Sonnet en i," like the one in x, reads as an allegory of writing. It models certain aspects of the predicament of signification as dictated by the nature of language. These poems are puissant because of their aptitude not to say anything definite but to evoke the indefinite—and to do so adhering always to the concrete, with extreme concision and precision, through powerfully particular, cuttingly sharp images. Moving from the indefinite and infinite continuum of all meaning, signification pins meaning down to cruelly finite and delimited terms. The undefined, unconfined aspiration of the swan ("cygne") or sign ("signe") that is pinned down to material elements finds in this sonnet both powerful dramatization and an iconic image.

    The main argument of "Le vierge, le vivace et le bel aujourd'hui" might be described as a depiction of signification as entrapment. Mallarmé's interest as a poet always turns to what escapes signification—or to what

---

10 Trans. A. S. Kline from Stéphane Mallarmé, *Un Coup de Dés & Other Poems* (poetryintranslation.com). Accessed 9/10/2025.

remains irremediably recalcitrant to signification in the midst of language's signifying activity. The poem presents the drama of a "cygne" ("swan") struggling to free itself from biting ice and fly off, but imaginably also of the exactly homophonous "signe" ("sign") structured so as to defeat its purpose of flying to any genuinely other space, a world beyond determinate, concrete reference. Such an other world is typically conjured up by signification as an order of the signified that is other to the world of immediate sensation in the signifier. But this other space is unreachable, or proves to be necessarily empty, a Nothing, at least in objective, empirical terms. The whole world of meaning reduces to nothing when considered in strictly material terms. Consequently, the swan remains mired in matter, and the signifiers that *should* serve as vehicles for its flight and liberation turn instead into shackles binding and freezing it in the ice.

As already remarked, the "Sonnet in i" uses an acute vowel sound "i" in order to give every line a lift—each line points upwards and aspires to take off into a separate, higher realm through the "i" at its end. The iconic shape of this letter embodies vertical thrust in the letter's main erect column topped by a discrete, *separate* point (the dot on the i) placed above it in a position of transcendence. The shrill, high-frequency sound of this graphic symbol, furthermore, is a phonetic equivalent (Iə) for clear, bright flight.

The swan's will to fly, to become a pure flash or sparkle of light ("pur éclat") by liberating itself from the world below and from any material significance or content (the signified meaning) is at the same time the linguistic, or more exactly the poetic, sign's aspiration to become a pure signifier detached from any delimiting, signified content. Hence the crucial play on "swan" ("cygne") as homophonic in French with "sign" ("signe"). The sign is looking for a kind of plenitude through release from bondage in the concrete world. "Le vierge, le vivace et le bel aujourd'hui"—literally "The virgin, the vivacious, and the beautiful today"—would be the dawn of a time beyond (or before) signification (like Walter Benjamin's *Jetztzeit*), in which the swan or sign could free itself from everything restricting and binding it and fly to a free and open space of literature, where everything can signify everything else, as in the symbolist poem. The homophonic identity of *signe* and *cygne* in French makes the swan a perfect symbol and mascot for the *symbolistes*' game-changing reworking of the logic of signification in language.

Already Baudelaire's "swan" in "Le Cygne" ("The Swan"), wandering forlorn over the rudely, rapidly developing landscape of modern Paris, in which it finds itself out of place, plays on the double-entendre of cygne/signe to suggest that this swan is a sign or trace and an allegory of the structural exile inherent to the condition of language itself. The language of signs is per se a space of exile. For Mallarmé, furthermore, "spacing," in a sense something like that developed by Blanchot ("espacement"), is constitutive of this exile. Even the boundaries which define exile are erased by spacing. The swan's being transformed from Baudelaire's allegorical symbol to a pure, white, blank space by Mallarmé is emblematic of the sign's emptying itself of content and becoming purely arbitrary. However, this process can never be quite complete. The mighty, but impossible, struggle to escape being enmired in fixed or frozen meanings is the drama depicted in this poem.

A mad poetic stroke of a drunken wing ("un coup d'aile ivre") threatens to shatter the frozen lake that is haunted by the transparent glacier of flights that have not flown ("Ce lac dur oublié que hante sous le givre / Le transparent glacier des vols qui n'ont pas fui"). The forgotten memory of a possibility of absolute signification still haunts the swan/sign in its entrapment within ordinary signification. The swan/sign still remembers itself as magnificent in the freedom it has always been deprived of, but which nonetheless haunts from birth the sign/swan's aptitude for—and stunted vocation to—the absolute. Despite this remembrance, the swan/sign is still without hope because of not having sung the region where it could (hypothetically) live ("Pour n'avoir pas chanté la région où vivre"). Instead, it has been enslaved to pragmatic purposes of signification of worldly objects—the sterile winter of boredom ("ennui") to which its heaven-seeking gleam is condemned ("Quand du stérile hiver a resplendi l'ennui").

In an imaginable revolt, and in its agony (like the midnight anguish represented in "Ses purs ongles" and in *Igitur*), the sign/swan would shake off this imprisonment. Being in truth indeterminate or "white," the sign/swan cannot be apprehended in any intellectual or conceptual (subject-object) operation but only in the immediacy of "white anguish" ("Tout son col secouera cette blanche agonie"). Still, the bird can deny whatever limiting space is inflicted upon it ("Par l'espace infligé à l'oiseau qui le nie"), but it cannot shake off the "horror" of the ground in which its plumage is frozen fast ("Mais non l'horreur du sol où le plumage est pris"). As an inescapable semiological fact, every sign is inextricably rooted in some species of material being that poses resistance to the absolute (non)significance (equivalent to the unlimited potential to be omni-significant) to which signs aspire. This fact of the sensory rootedness of their meaning imprisons and mires signs in matter.

The swan's very whiteness or purity condemns it to this condition of immobility, which it endures defiantly with its cold dream of contempt ("songe froid du mépris") caught in this "useless exile" ("l'exile inutile"). The swan's exile, as already indicated, points back to Baudelaire's "Le Cygne" (which begins with and returns to the emblematic figure of Andromache in exile), a precursor of this swan/sign, whose experience is now articulated with vastly intensified reflective resonances rendering more explicit some of the fateful tensions and limits inherent in the structural semiotics of the sign as a condition of exile. Some further aspects of the life and death of the sign are explored in Mallarmé's banner poem, "L'après-midi d'un faune," of which we will consider a few passages bearing on the function of signs as symbols in the *symboliste* sense. The impossible relation to an externality becomes the fecundating feature of the immanent life-and-death struggle of the sign.

"L'après-midi d'un faune"

Excerpt from "L'après-midi d'un faune"

Inerte, tout brûle dans l'heure fauve
Sans marquer par quel art ensemble détala
Trop d'hymen souhaité de qui cherche le la :
Alors m'éveillerai-je à la ferveur première,
Droit et seul, sous un flot antique de lumière,
Lys ! et l'un de vous tous pour l'ingénuité.

Inert, all things burn in the tawny hour
Not seeing by what art there fled away together
Too much of hymen desired by one who seeks there
The natural A: then I'll wake to the primal fever
Erect, alone, beneath the ancient flood, light's power,
Lily! And the one among you all for artlessness.[11]

The valorization of the qualities of the signifier entails a relative emancipation from the dictatorship of the signified as determining prosaic meaning. The status of the representational object is placed radically into question by Mallarmé's poetry, and this can be illustrated by one of Mallarmé's most characteristic poems, "L'après-midi d'un faune." The poem adumbrates a plot concerning the faun's purported seduction of two nymphs. But the faun is doubting whether his *jouissance* may not all be only within his own imaginary representation and specifically within language. Is there anything which is not immanent to language in what he experiences? Is there any truth to his experience, or is it all purely subjective impression, alias "literature"? Is there

---

11 Translation by A. S. Kline from https://www.poemhunter.com/poem/l-apres-midi-d-un-faune/.

any real object or referent to the mimesis he delivers in his poetic narrative? That narrative is internally articulated. It is marked as incorrigibly double. It is structured by a double marking whereby the fiction marks *itself* as fiction. This double marking sets up a wholly immanent system of difference within the poem itself and without direct relation to any externality. This structure constitutes a realization of the "ideal" status of the faun's "fault," his sensual excess, and a token of the nature of his experience as a trace immanent to signification rather than referring to any presence outside it.

The nature of the faun's language, most typically a kind of song or poetry, seems itself to dictate that he can experience only language and hence the feminine as just the "la" in the phrase "who seeks the *la*" ("qui cherche le la")—a generic, universal femininity marked by the gendered definite article used to refer to anything feminine.[12] His "hymen" (the membrane ruptured by first sex) or coitus is consummated only in his backing off from the act of ravishment and finding himself in a state of solitude and indeed virginity ("Mon sein, vierge de preuve"). The focus on virginity again here picks up from "Herodiade" as a recurrent obsession. The faun's virginity is the sexually sterile state of language made pure by becoming purely self-referential and at least apparently cut off from contact with any world or object outside language. This is immediate, onanistic sexuality. Compared to it, the nymphs are "too much sex," or more euphemistically "hymen" ("Trop d'hymen"), for whoever seeks a more immediate consummation bypassing union with the other sex.

The faun's experience is fundamentally one of undecidability. Between the erotic and the artistic, between the sexual and the solitary, his doubts "achieving themselves" in "many subtle ramifications" become the expression of his essential state, namely, that of the poet. It is a state of being in between animal nature and human, as well as a state of "hymen" signaling the membrane between virginity and sex. This is because he turns all reality into language (just as, *in nuce*, the swan ("cygne") becomes sign). Symbolist language is precisely this medium, this in-between with no outside, no real reference to a presence that would render things decidable. The logic of signification, based on a real difference between sign and referent, signifier and signified, breaks down when we enter fully into the experience of linguisticality. As Jacques Derrida perceived, "That which is thus removed [by the hymen] is not difference itself but the different, the

---

12 The "la," of course, also signifies the sixth tone, "A," of the seven-tone diatonic scale. This is the penultimate moment where melodic motion turns inward in moving toward resolution and completion in the final, seventh tone.

differing, the decidable exteriority of different things" ("Ce qui est ainsi levé [par le hymen], ce n'est donc pas la différence mais le différent, les différents, l'extériorité décidable des différents").[13]

The referential object is represented in the poem as a sexual object. Sensually concrete *jouissance*, rather than only words, would be the other of (or to) language, the extra-linguistic object par excellence. Yet, since artistic language is itself an object of *jouissance* and even insists upon foregrounding all the sensuously concrete qualities of language, the faun is perplexed as to whether his experience is really of extra-linguistic "nymphs," that is, women, females, or is rather purely an artistic experience emerging from his flute and, in fact, immanent to his own language and song. In this case, it would be an object that is not distinct from his narration, a referent that is nothing but the effect of his linguistic act of referring and having no existence independently of it. The faun is not certain that this is so: he only doubts whether his ravishment may have been no more than his own dream or artistic invention. In the narration of the poem, then, he actually produces an artwork that could itself produce exactly the experience of sensual longing and "almost-love" that it represents and is about as having happened. This pure fantasy *could* also be the case.

The undecidability of whether the love act or attempt has actually transpired anywhere but in the narration of the poem—and this is what the faun himself, in effect, is asking all throughout—belongs to the very character of language as this poem reveals it. The faun's musings constitute an acute theoretical and lyrical reflection on this epistemological problem.

Undecidability Rather than Suppression of Reference

Second Excerpt from "L'après-midi d'un faune"

Aimai-je un rêve ?
Mon doute, amas de nuit ancienne, s'achève
En maint rameau subtil, qui, demeuré les vrais
Bois même, prouve, hélas ! que bien seul je m'offrais
Pour triomphe la faute idéale de roses.

Did I love a dream?
My doubt, mass of ancient night, ends extreme
In many a subtle branch, that remaining the true

---

13 Jacques Derrida, *la dissémination* (Paris: Seuil, 1972), 259.

Woods themselves, proves, alas, that I too
Offered myself, alone, as triumph, the false ideal of roses.

The inescapable linguisticality of the faun's experience is brought forth not by definitive elimination of the referent but only by its undecidability. This suspense, as a constitutive gap between signifier and signified, or word and object, belongs to the character of language as, in its nature, referential.[14] If there were no gesture of referring at all, then neither would there be language; the entrapment of the faun would not be in language but merely in the sensory titillations of sounds that are no words. But language alone cannot decide upon its referent. Its action of referring remains from the point of view of language alone undecidable as to whether it is true or false. One might think that the answer can be found out easily enough by looking beyond language to facts. But the undecidability of reference on the basis of language alone, the fact that it produces a possibility which it cannot decide, a possibility which in fact therefore produces *it* as undecidable, characterizes language in an essential way. And this character has unlimited importance for poetry and for Mallarmé. It means that language per se, the poet's one proper concern qua poet, is not bound by any referents and that its essence as language lies elsewhere—in the play of suggestions, phonic and iconic, as well as semantic, that it produces.

When language is no longer conceived of as essentially determined in its meaning by an external referent, as is the case especially for poetic language, at least as Mallarmé understands it, then it becomes essentially undecidable as to its meaning. This is the realization that the faun comes to and emblematizes. It is also what Derrida has worked out critically on a theoretical plane. In literature and life alike, the referent can always be specified only through further language: it never becomes purely present without linguistic mediation, as Derrida has repeatedly attempted to show, starting from his analyses of reference as indication and expression in Husserl's phenomenology.[15] Thus, the model of sign and referent gives place to the trace, which has no pre-given referent and is itself the origin of an undecidable *possibility* of reference. Reference is not *excluded*, but reference to the empirical world no longer fixes and exhausts meaning, as in the pragmatist view of language in which meaning is reduced to its use function in relation to an externally posited world of objects.

---

14 This thesis is developed in marvelous detail and subtlety by Hans-Jost Frey, *Studien über das Reden der Dichter* (München: Fink, 1986), 13–53.
15 Derrida, *La voix et le phénomène (Introduction au problème du signe dans la phénoménologie de Husserl)* (Paris: Presses Universitaires de France, 1967).

The undecidability of reference, such as it is dramatized by the faun, receives extended analysis from Derrida in his reading of Mallarmé's "Mimique."[16] There is reference in the mime's gestures, but without any real or external referent, which is to say that the gesture of reference remains—and necessarily—without any simply given referent that could finally decide *to what* reference is being made. For Derrida, the important thing is that meaning becomes purely differential. Following principles established by Saussurian linguistics, for signifiers to be differentiated, they must be assigned different referential values. Reference is thus a necessary projection from the production of sense by difference that is constitutive of language. But if reference is generated purely by a difference between signifiers, the actual existence of the referent is undecidable from within language itself. The structure of reference must be there in so far as it belongs to the character of language as a differential system. Yet, considered rigorously, reference is *produced* by signifying and thus cannot ground it. Reference belongs to the play of signification, and indeed the faun has made it play into his poetic musing as the uncertainty leading and animating his whole tale. He asks himself whether the nymphs exist at all outside of his own fantasy and desire?

Like the gestures of the mime in Mallarmé's "Mimique," so also the poet's expressions in the theatre of Derrida's essay "La double séance" play the role of "a reference without referent, without first or last unity, a phantom that is the phantom of no flesh, erring, without past, without death, without birth or presence" ("une référence sans référent, sans unité première ou dernière, fantôme qui n'est fantôme d'aucune chair, errant, sans passé, sans mort, sans naissance ni presence," 255). Mimed gestures, like poetry, originate the fluid, virtual world to which they refer.

Derrida is saying that representation has no grounding in a being that would be something else besides representation. Every signified is itself already a signifier: language reaches and produces always only more language. Yet Derrida said in an interview (and particularly regarding the phrase "il n'y a pas de hors texte") that his work does not imply that "there is nothing outside the text" or language but rather the exact opposite.[17] In fact, his attending to the self-deconstructing dynamics of language can show its nullity and leave everything that counts "beyond language." The "call of the Other" ("l'appel de l'autre") emerges as Derrida's imperious passion and irrepressible obsession. In these terms, some of the leading ideas broached by Mallarmé have been worked out in further detail and philosophical depth by Derrida.

---

16 Derrida, "La double séance," *La dissémination*, 215–346.
17 Derrida, *Positions* (Paris: Minuit, 1972), 80–90.

The self-reflexive, autotelic nature of language in particular is unveiled in its paradoxical and (I would say) prophetic orientation toward an Other, even an absolute, ungraspable Other sometimes figured as divine.

Mallarmé expressly orients writing to *"Something else* ...it seems that the scattered trembling of a page does not want anything but to delay and palpitate with impatience for the possibility of something else" (*"Autre chose... ce semble que l'épars frémissement d'une page ne veuille sinon surseoir ou palpite d'impatience, à la possibilité d'autre chose,"* "La musique et les lettres," 647). He writes of a beyond, an *au-delà* that is "the agent and motor" of every fiction exercising "a superior attraction as of a void" ("une attirance supérieur comme d'un vide," 647).

Meanderings of Chance from *Igitur* to *Un coup de dés*

In elucidating *Un coup de dés*'s originality, R. Howard Bloch recreates the day-by-day ambience of Mallarmé's domestic life and social world as a context for the poem. He casts surprising light on the work's minute particulars. The resulting disclosures tend to shatter membranes between text and context.[18] Bloch indicates one direction in which Derrida's reading deconstructing reference can be extended through making referential context interpenetrate with the textual signifiers of the poem rather than standing on its own outside them. A kind of deconstruction of ordinary assumptions about referential reality as independent of the language through which we apprehend it is performed by Mallarmé's sketch for his "grand oeuvre," his "Coup de dés." Such assumptions can find their philosophical charter in logical positivism, with its grounding of all truth in supposedly solid, unambiguous empirical fact as simply given.

Un coup de dés by eliminating syntax eliminates logic. The universe breaks open to unmasterable chance. Not being susceptible of being suppressed by logic, chance ("le hasard") has won the battle. Mallarmé had outlined this problematic already early on in *Igitur*, his uncompleted metaphysical drama. Igitur's act is itself a shake of the dice. He "simply shakes the dice—movement, before going to rejoin the ashes, the atoms of his ancestors" ("Igitur secoue simplement les dés—mouvement, avant d'aller rejoinder les cendres, atomes de ses ancêtres," 442). His breath, "which contained chance," wavers in his very last act, the act of suicide itself. As is said at the beginning of Act IV, "Briefly, in an act where chance is in play, chance always accomplishes its

---

18 R. Howard Bloch, *One Toss of the Dice: The Incredible Story of How a Poem Made Us Modern* (New York: Norton, 2016).

own Idea in affirming or negating itself" ("Bref dans un acte où le hasard est en jeu, c'est toujours le hasard qui accomplit sa propre Idée en s'affirmant ou se niant," 441). Igitur therefore finds the act itself useless ("inutile"), and he simply lays down in the tomb of his ancestors.

The act of the subject does not constrain chance. "Chance always realizes itself and accomplishes its own Idea." In face of chance or randomness, the subject's affirmation or negation founders ("Bref dans un acte où le hasard est en jeu, c'est toujours le hasard qui accomplit sa propre Idée en s'affirmant ou se niant. Devant son existence la négation et l'affirmation viennent échouer," 441). Nonetheless, the personal act abandoned to chance permits the infinite to exist ("permet à l'Infini d'être," 441) and fixes it in form ("que l'Infini est enfin *fixé*," 442). By throwing himself open to chance, the subject manages to reduce the infinite to something actually existing. "He reduces chance to the Infinite, which he says must exist somewhere" ("il réduit le hasard à l'*Infini*— qui, dit-il, doit exister quelque part," 442). The "Argument" at the beginning had said that "the infinite issues from chance, which you have negated" ("L'infini sort du hasard, que vous avez nié," 434). The act of negation issues in the infinite, which is thereby given to exist as a form, releasing it from mere chance. The negation of oneself by suicide fails in itself to annihilate all chance, but it produces a form of infinity for all eternity concerning oneself, namely, death, in which there is no possibility, no contingency.

According to a widely accepted critical current, *Igitur* serves as a psychological introduction to the *Grand Oeuvre*. Its central idea is that "no human act can abolish the fact of human contingency."[19] Thomas Williams defines the dilemma produced by this predicament as follows: "In *Un coup de dés* Mallarmé is writing of absolute knowledge, of the necessity which he feels— and the impossibility in which he finds himself—of transcending in his art the realm of 'number-ideas'" (82). Embodying in poetry the "idées-nombres" as the ideal Pythagorean order in the universe, and thereby perfectly uniting form (number) and meaning (idea) in an expression of the absolute, would be to transcend human contingency. This, indeed, is what Mallarmé aims at in his poetry. Poetry would thus regain what myth the world over, from the Egyptian Book of the Dead to Polynesian creation legend, envisages as a state before the separation of Earth and Sky, before the emergence of the world and consciousness from Nothing, from the undifferentiated unity of the womb, the primordial, amniotic sea of chaos. Symbolically, this state is often represented by the ouroboros serpent devouring its own tail in an

---

19 Thomas A. Williams, *Mallarmé and the Language of Mysticism* (Athens: University of Georgia Press, 1970), 83.

eternal circle. Paradoxically, however, and contrary to Hegel's affirmation of absolute knowing, Mallarmé discovers that it is only in stating the *impossibility* of such a necessary and perfect work of art that it can be humanly achieved.

The chance that Mallarmé speaks of not being able to eliminate in *Coup de dés* is, among other things, the chance that makes words mean things wholly unsuited to their physical make-up, particularly their sound. The "coup de dés," or "toss of the dice," after all, is a figure for writing or for poetry, which tries to create a necessary structure, as does every work of art, out of words determined arbitrarily (at least in a secular view) by chance. The poet's use of words is always a playing with chance like dice in the attempt to express the absolute Idea. The constellations of stars represent this randomly strewn yet mysteriously destined character of a universe in which all the elements are relationally defined. Poetic language is a kind of constellation of concrete elements that all reflect on one another. In "Hérodiade," exemplarily, this technique produces the constellated consonances of *or, sonore, doré, dévoré, ignorée*.

Poetic language, distinguished essentially as verse, consists in "the ensemble of relations existing in all, Music" ("l'ensemble des rapports existant dans tout, la Musique," "Crise de vers," 368). Such an ensemble of relations can be represented visually as well as musically. For Mallarmé, words in verse "ignite themselves by reciprocal reflections as a virtual train of fires on precious jewels, replacing the respiration perceptible in the ancient lyric inspiration or the personal, enthusiastic management of the phrase" ("s'allument de reflets réciproques comme une virtuelle traînée de feux sur des pierreries, remplaçant la respiration perceptible en l'ancien souffle lyrique ou la direction personnelle enthousiaste de la phrase," 366). Letting these relations speak for themselves, Mallarmé abandons the inspired personal voice of the prophetic poetry of his Romantic predecessors and replaces it with a new, impersonal kind of transcendence belonging to "the pure notion" ("la notion pure," 368). Yet this inspiration from beyond individual subjects and their intentions actually makes poetry realize rather than relinquish its vocation to a kind of prophetic revelation reaching beyond the merely human.

The autonomous and inner determination of language by its elements on a purely internal relational basis is of the utmost importance in Mallarmé's conception of poetry. The verse, with its artfully chosen arrangement of words, is the poet's attempt to neutralize chance. In Mallarmé's cryptic, but exquisite formulation: "An ordering of the book of verse emerges inborn or everywhere and eliminates chance" ("Une ordonnance du livre de vers poind innée ou partout, élimine le hasard," "Crise de vers," 366). Yet this system is always projected by Mallarmé as collapsing toward its own origin. The moment of catastrophe, immediately before the traces appear on the page, which witness to it, fascinates him most intensely. However, this origin in language is at least partly human, dependent on a subject ("un sujet, fatal," 366) and thus fraught with contingency.

The constellations are not merely a system of signs from which, strictly considered, the diachronic dimension is erased, as in a certain Saussurian model of language as a purely relational, synchronic system. They exist for a subject in time. The relationality of language is not a positive, self-subsistent structure but rather the testimony of the nothingness at its core corresponding to the human substrate (the subject) conditioned by chance. The poet, as this human instance, consciously takes up "the reigning language, first to tune it according to its origin, so that an august sense is produced: in Verse, dispenser and orderer of the play of the pages, master of the book" ("le langage régnant, d'abord à l'accorder selon son origine, pour qu'un sens auguste produisît : en le Vers, dispensateur, ordonnateur du jeu des pages, maître du livre," "Étalages," 375). This masterful order of Verse converts chance into a necessary blank or silence: "chance conquered word by word, indefectibly the blank returns, once gratuitous, now certain, to conclude that nothing lies beyond and to authenticate silence" ("le hasard vaincu mot par mot, indéfectiblement le blanc revient, tout à l'heure gratuit, certain maintenant, pour conclure que rien au-delà et authentiquer le silence," "Le mystère dans les lettres," 387).

Language is full of intricate interrelations, yet with only chance at their origin. Art strives to convert this indeterminacy into the necessity of the Idea. Mallarmé's idealism, in this respect, is analogous to Hegel's. He attempts to achieve on an aesthetic plane the Absolute that Hegel had philosophized as the end and totalization of his philosophy of history. But Mallarmé, together with his poststructuralist interpreters, is obsessed also with the impossibility of totalization.

Mallarmé sees language's original and true state as whole and as saturated with everything that appears subsequently under specific, partial forms of actual discourse and expression. For Mallarmé, the emptying of language is a poetic technique aimed at experiencing its plenitude. In his vision, poetry is present in the highest degree in the original fact of language per se long before becoming manifest in any of its deliberate artifices devised by poetic art. And he conceives of poetic art in the broadest, most inclusive terms. He maintains that "in truth there is no prose: there is the alphabet and then verses that are more or less strict: more or less diffuse. Every time there is an effort of style, there is versification" ("Mais, en vérité, il n'y a pas de prose : il y a l'alphabet et puis des vers plus ou moins serrés : plus ou moins diffus. Toutes les fois qu'il y a effort au style, il y a versification").

The absolute Idea can be achieved only by enacting the absolute negation that language is at its origin. Mallarmé encapsulates this principle in his picturesque, consummately crafted pronouncement: "I say: a flower! and outside of the forgetting to which my voice relegates any contour as something else besides the known calices, there arises musically, the very idea and suave, the one absent from all bouquets" ("Je dis : une fleur ! et, hors de l'oubli où ma voix relègue aucun contour, en tant que quelque chose d'autre que les calices sus, musicalement se lève, idée même et suave, l'absente de tous bouquets," "Crise de vers," 368). This negation intrinsic to language involves also the disappearance of the poet as the origin and anchor of speech. The poet disappears poetically in and through the act of elocution ("disparition élocutoire du poète," 366). Mallarmé takes the negation of the author and even of human consciousness to an extreme in "Igitur." But there is a limit: consciousness must eliminate itself in order to eliminate chance, for it is always embedded in a present time with its contingencies, not in the absolute Midnight (*Minuit*), where frozen past and negated future are fully certain and fixed. To finally fix the Idea, consciousness must eliminate itself. And yet, that very act of elimination, as an act of consciousness, has an element of chance: it is not completely necessary but rather an act of will, a choice inevitably influenced by contingencies.

Un coup de dés is Mallarmé's attempt to make chance itself into a work by enacting it in and through thought in the poem. Yet all thought emits chance ("Toute Pensée émet un Coup de Dés," 477), even in the act of extinguishing itself. The poem, by its art, attempts to annihilate not just chance but even time and eventuality, reducing them to pure place in the poem, a constellation of words on the page: "NOTHING [...] WILL HAVE TAKEN PLACE [...] BUT THE PLACE [...] EXCEPT FOR [...] PERHAPS [...] A CONSTELLATION" ("RIEN N'AURA EU LIEU [...] QUE LE LIEU [...] EXCEPTÉ [...] PEUT-ÊTRE [...] UNE CONSTELLATION"). Mallarmé aims to create ex nihilo, outside time and its chain of consequences, a purely formal structure. His poem's unique and revolutionary layout emphasizes the simultaneous vision of the page. Each page is like a letter expanded. The work is readable only as expressive of an idea of poetry and literature rather than for its represented contents. It must be read as embodying concretely and impersonally this universal ideal of art or beauty and not as a communication from someone. The initiative is thus ceded to the words themselves ("Crise du Vers," 366).

Gerald Bruns suggests that "typography was to replace syntax as a way of establishing relationships among words." In this displacement, Bruns explains, "Syntactical structures are everywhere to be found but they are radically diffused by the way the words are positioned on the page" (115). This entails a subordination (if not the elimination) of syntax, which describes movement in time, to relations in space. But the principle of ordered relations among words remains intact as the rule of poetry.

Michel Murat views Mallarmé's *grand oeuvre* as a revolutionary refashioning of the verse, giving it a new standing as a new beginning for a foundationless poetry. He shows how Mallarmé reinvents the verse, taking it from the classic alexandrine into the age of free verse and prose-poetry, by inventing a new genre that relates the verse to his conception of the book. Certainly, the visual form, including typography and choreography of the text on the page, takes on a new life in this new form envisaging an ideal and absolute Number. The disposition in double pages, for example, reformulates in another dimension the principle of the caesura (the break in the middle) that is constitutive for the traditional alexandrine verse.

Dismantling syntax, freeing words and their force from its constraints, is an interesting experiment. Nevertheless, the force and significance of words was always, in fact, in good part, produced by syntax, among the other integrative resources of language. Undoing the connecting structures of language releases certain energies, but they are energies that are there thanks only to the disciplined work of constructing meaningful structures out of coherent linguistic materials. And so this energy is itself borrowed from what is being demolished.

Suppressing syntax makes words stand out on their own ("l'isolement de la parole," "Crise de vers," 368) as immediate presences. This, however, serves also as a way of evoking absence and making it present in the mode both of the visual blank and of an auditory mode of silence ("le poème tu, aux blancs," 367). These techniques become crucial to Mallarmé's *grand oeuvre*, even more than anything at the level of representation of referential contents in words, which he programmatically abandons as secondary and as not belonging to the true nature and vocation of art. His theoretical statements from "Crise de vers" to "Ballets" harp on this presencing of absence. And overcoming representation forms a pillar for the interpretation of his work by Jacques Rancière and by the many philosophers and critics who are subsequently influenced by him, including Quentin Meillassoux.[20]

In opening especially to non-representational channels of poetic communication, the "Coup de dés" does not completely abandon the conventional structure of the statement. It still employs complete sentences

---

20 Meillassoux, *Le Nombre et la sirène : Un déchiffrage du "Coup de dés" de Mallarmé* (Paris: Fayard, 2011).

in larger type—but as discontinuous and as dispersed across the surface of its pages. In effect, this poem opens syntax up to all the many incompatible possibilities of thought that jostle together and are inevitably eliminated and reduced in order to produce the closure of the statement. Mallarmé's open form of an exploded verse (*vers éclaté*) now accommodates these competing countercurrents and makes them swim together in the sea of the text.

The poem displays "carefully modulated mobility controlled by the white space, which, like silence in music, intervenes to give the line a formal as against a strictly linguistic intelligibility" (Bruns, 116). "One has to imagine a visual experience of music, the movement of free, visible forms, in order to comprehend fully what Mallarmé seeks to achieve" (*ibid.*, 116).

Bruns highlights the fact that "Mallarmé attaches a great premium to the written or printed word—the word not as a functional element in a discourse but as an object existing in a spatial and visual field" (109). "[F]or Mallarmé poetry lays claim to the domain of music by way of the written word, which belongs not to sound but to space [...] [the] present task of modern poetry is to find a way of transposing the symphony to the book [...] the true source of music must not be the elemental sound of brasses, strings, or wood-winds, but the intellectual and written word in all its glory—music of perfect fullness and clarity—the totality of universal relationships" (110, cf. end of "Crise de vers," 367–68).

In the midst of this universal diapason, silence, the blank, is the presence of Nothingness, and this is Beauty. Writing gives form to silence by its moving arabesques upon the page (Mallarmé, "La musique et les lettres," 648). Through "the sensation of absolute emptiness," our minds "partake of thought." Bruns concludes: "Mallarmé's vision, then, is one of the transcendent word—of language which belongs neither to the world of things nor to the human world of speech but rather to primordial emptiness, in which the splendor of beauty exists as a sheer presence, a pure quality unpredicated of any reality but the word. Mallarmé's indeed is the song of Orpheus in his absence" (117).

Thomas Williams captures this paradoxical presence of nothingness succinctly: "Mallarmé uses the physical presence of words to evoke their contrary: the nothingness and silence of the introspective void" (38). In this interior nothingness is encountered the absoluteness of Being. "What Mallarmé accomplishes is not so much a transformation of the object itself as of the quality of consciousness which apprehends it. And for this new consciousness, the object becomes, in its magic absence-in-presence, an upsurge into experience of absolute Being, mutely offering itself for our contemplation" (39).

Building on such interpretations, recent readings of Mallarmé have turned this absolutizing view of a linguistic metaphysics in a political direction. Following the impetus of Jacques Rancière in particular, especially recent philosophical readings of Mallarmé have attempted to assess the political implications and significance of the poet's aesthetic transfiguration of language as an act absolutizing social and personal being and destiny. I pursue this line of inquiry in a forthcoming companion volume where the current philosopher-critics are discussed in detail.[21] My focus in the present volume, however, remains on symbolism as an aesthetic experience and artistic technique.

---

21 *Mallarmé's Theo-Political Poetics: Revolution and Revelation in French Symbolist Poetry* (forthcoming from Cambridge University Press in Cambridge Elements: History of Philosophy and Theology in the West).

Chapter 3
SYMBOLIST MEANING AND SUBJECTIVE FEELING

I have argued that what counts in the word as symbol is what it *is* even more than what it conventionally signifies, and I have suggested how the material being of the signifier is exploited in myriad ways by symbolist poets to create the effects of meaning that are so peculiarly characteristic of symbolist poems. Another sort of immediately present being in the poetic process besides the word physically present as sound or graphic figure is the psychological state, the consciousness, of the one writing or reading the poem. It is not just the materiality of the signifier that can be exploited by the symbolist poet to extract sub-semantic meaning or a sense that is more immediate than the semantic content ascribed by linguistic convention to a verbal sign. To insist exclusively on language as material would be reductive, especially in view of the expansive development of the power of the word as pure ideality, as "la notion pure," found at the fountainhead of Mallarmé's symbolist poetry and poetics.

On the basis of the aesthetics of "effect" as inherited from Edgar Allen Poe, the French symbolists identified the essential and poetic meaning of a word with the *effect* it produces in a reader/auditor. Poe's "The Philosophy of Composition" (1846) explains how he composed his poem "The Raven" by calculating the effects to be produced by each word so as to contribute to the unity of effect of the composition as a whole on the reader's emotions.[1] The immediate impact of the word, the impression in which the word exists as a particular form and instance of subjective consciousness rather than abstractly as an element in a system, is a type of being. It is being-in-time, considered phenomenologically. This dimension of language and existence is precisely what is in question in the aesthetics of effect as expressed, exemplarily, in Mallarmé's prescription for writing poetry: *"Paint not the thing but the effect it*

---

1 Poe, "The Philosophy of Composition," *Graham's Magazine* 28/4, April 1846, 163–167.

produces" ("*Peindre, non la chose, mais l'effet qu'elle produit*").[2] This formula, in some respects more than any other, serves to define the new poetics of symbolism.

The word must be considered always as a manifestation of a speaker (or writer or reader) in process of speech. The word as subjective expression may be considered as consisting in a linguistic surface that renders manifest an ontological depth. This is to accord the symbol an ontological dimension in the being of the subject, as well as in the being of language as such.

To plumb the being of language in its emotional and imaginative depths means examining and expressing what language means, even intimately, to whoever dwells in it. Such meaning as this can never be contained within an abstract, objective system of differences. It is radically personal and subjective in its purport—although to express it is precisely to objectify it and, in a certain sense, render it accessible to someone else. Edmund Wilson defined symbolist poetry as an attempt "to communicate unique personal feeling" (*Axel's Castle*, 4). Such a communication of radically subjective experience is wont to proceed by "allusion" and "suggestion" and, in any case, by some form of analogy.

Symbolism's avenue of approach to the perception of universal analogy is via the particular sensations of the individual subject. Baudelaire stresses this point in his critical (and occasional) writings, which are of one accord with the exquisitely unique and personally charged perceptions reflected in his poems. Writing under the ensign of imagination as "The Queen of the Faculties" ("La Reine des Facultés"), he argues that individual perception and "sensibilité" are the basis of true art: "The artist, the true artist, the true poet must paint only according to what he sees and feels. He must be *really* faithful to his own nature. He must avoid like death borrowing the eyes and sentiments of another man, however great he may be, because then the productions he gives us would be relative to him lies and not *realities*." ("L'artiste, le vrai artiste, le vrai poète, ne doit peindre que selon qu'il voit et qu'il sent. Il doit être *réellement* fidèle à sa propre nature. Il doit éviter comme la mort d'emprunter les yeux et les sentiments d'un autre homme, si grand qu'il soit; car alors les productions qu'il nous donnerait seraient, relativement à lui, des mensonges, et non des *réalités*.").[3]

The emphasis of the original text falls twice heavily on the assertion of the reality of the poet's peculiar perceptions. Baudelaire insists that they are the artist's avenue to truth, reversing the epistemological bias in favor of what can be confirmed by other observers and the criterion of experimental science,

---

[2] Letter to Cazalis, October 30, 1864, *Œuvres complètes* (1998), I, 663.

[3] Baudelaire, "Salon de 1859," in *Œuvres complètes* (Paris: Gallimard, 1954), 773.

namely, that valid observations must be repeatable and even reproducible. By refining the hermeneutics of his own subjectivity in order to express his most intimate feelings, idiosyncratic fantasies and individual perceptions and sensations, the poet grows in his capacity to articulate being analogically, the being to which science is blind and which mass society drowns out. This precisely is authentic, passionate, living being, and therefore all that concerns poetry and makes it poignant.

Baudelaire shows himself to be a symbolist by his effort to grasp all reality and unreality through aesthetic experience. A symbol of his, like his mistress's hair in "La chevelure," enfolds whole universes.

> La langoureuse Asie et la brûlante Afrique,
> Tout un monde lointain, absent, presque défunt,
> Vit dans tes profondeurs, forêt aromatique !
> Comme d'autres esprits voguent sur la musique,
> Le mien, ô mon amour ! nage sur ton parfum.

> Languorous Asia and burning Africa,
> A whole distant world, absent and nearly defunct,
> Lives in your depths, aromatic forest!
> As other spirits sail on music,
> Mine, oh my love, swims on your perfume.

That these worlds of allusive reference should be far off and absent, almost dead (lointain, absent, presque défunt), suggests the symbol's potency to revive and presence the world outside ordinary human experience, which is so restrictively structured for convenience and safety, screening out the depths and the forest of the real. Worlds of the past, which are temporally absent worlds, can also be recovered from the symbol of the hair:

> Extase ! Pour peupler ce soir l'alcôve obscure
> Des souvenirs dormant dans cette chevelure,
> Je la veux agiter dans l'air comme un mouchoir !

> Ecstasy! To populate this evening's dark alcove
> Of memories dormant in this hair,
> I want to shake it in the air like a handkerchief!

The speaker's ecstasy and his erotic elation and involvement with his mistress's hair constitute an essential condition of the symbol, namely, emotional, existential investment on the part of the subject for whom it is symbolic.

The "profondeurs" or depths of a word or object like a woman's hair in "La chevelure" are to be found in an existential depth that unfolds around such an object in dynamic relation with other things through the existential subject. The hair is inexhaustible not merely as an object but also as a manifestation within the universal analogical relation of being. The hair occasions an experience of the essentially erotic which relates—reaching infinitely beyond the experience of one specific object—to "the force that through the green fuse drives the flower," as Dylan Thomas put it, or to what "inwardly holds the universe together" ("was die Welt im Innersten zusammenhält") in the idiom of Goethe's Faust.

This principle characterizes *symbolisme* in France and Belgium as a late phase in the evolution of poetry that realizes the art in its purest state. The speaker stresses his *personal* experience of the hair as his love fetish and distills this into an olfactory perception, making it purely a sensation without objective form in space, purely a subjective impression. Baudelaire insists that the hair contains all reality but that it is experienced in the most subjective of states of consciousness, like a dream:

Tu contiens, mer d'ébène, un éblouissant rêve [...].
(You contain, sea of ebony, a dazzling dream [...].)

The exquisiteness of his peculiar sensations opens infinite worlds through the so-called "secondary qualities" that, according to empiricist epistemology, do not exist in things themselves at all but only in subjects' modes of perceiving them.

À grands flots de parfum, le son et la couleur [...].
(In great streams of perfume, the sound and color [...].)

Baudelaire had already privileged secondary qualities such as color, smell, and sound in "Les Correspondances" ("les parfums, les couleurs et les sons"), as well as throughout his lyrics, since the reality they convey is irreducibly subjective and often personal and passionate. And he requires his readers to encounter these dimensions of being for themselves. This accent on pure sensation is not indulgence in purely and merely subjective impressions but rather a method for meeting up with the deeper sense of the real that refuses to yield itself to standardized modes of perceiving and to rational analysis. Mallarmé confides that he "arrived at the Idea of the Universe by sensation alone" ("je suis arrive à l'Idée de l'Univers par la seule sensation," Letter to Villiers, September 24, 1867). He experiences "the sensation of absolute emptiness" ("la sensation du vide absolu," *ibid.*, 724) and writes on multiple occasions of his sensuous encounter with Nothingness as the metaphysical experience founding his sense of true reality.

In the line of Romantic thinking that we have seen Mallarmé developing to its Symbolist apogee, poetry provides the essential sensorial means to know the universe and express human existence. In Mallarmé's "stammering" definition: "Poetry is the expression, by human language brought back to its essential rhythm, of the mysterious sense of the aspects of existence: thus it endows our sojourn with authenticity and constitutes the sole spiritual task" ("La poésie est l'expression, par le langage humain ramené à son rythme essentiel, du sens mystérieux des aspects de l'existence : elle doue ainsi d'authenticité notre séjour et constitue la seule tâche spirituelle," Lettre à Léo D'Orfer, 27 juin 1884, 782).

Baudelaire's claims for the imagination, namely, that "it creates the world" ("elle a crée le monde"), even in a religious sense ("on peut bien dire cela, je crois, même dans un sens religieux"), and that "imagination is the queen of the realm of truth" ("l'imagination est la reine du vrai") rehearse familiar Romantic postulates animated by revolt against the prosaic world of fact imposed by the dawning industrial age.[4] But, by the time of Mallarmé and Rimbaud, the idea of the Romantic individual protesting in his integrity against a corrupt and blind society will be outmoded. The individual per se will tend to implode like a hollow shell. Mallarmé declares the "elocutionary disappearance of the poet" ("disparition élocutoire du poète") and the need to "cede the initiative to words" ("cède l'initiative aux mots," "Crise du Vers," 366), while Rimbaud attacks the "subjective poetry" ("poésie subjective") of Banville and other Parnassians in order to announce instead, stupefyingly, that "JE est un autre" ("I is an other"). He describes himself as being in a state of utter passivity with regard to his own psychic processes. "Si le cuivre s'eveille clarion, il n'y a rien de sa faute. Cela m'est évident : j'assiste à l'éclosion de ma pensée ; je la regarde et je l'écoute [...]." ("If the brass awakes as a trumpet, that is not its fault. This is evident to me: I observe the blooming of my own thought: I watch and listen to it [...]").[5]

Mallarmé's symbols in the early poems crystallize as reflections of his own poetic subjectivity, albeit reflections which are equally transfigurations such as had been provided by "La Beauté" of Baudelaire, in whose eyes poets saw themselves idealized, as in the reflections "Of pure mirrors that make all

---

4 Baudelaire, "Salon de 1859," in *Œuvres complètes*, 773 and 774.
5 Rimbaud, correspondence with Georges Izambard, May 13, 1871, and with Paul Dumay, May 15, 1871.

things more beautiful" ("De purs miroirs qui font toutes choses plus belles," "La Beauté"). One such symbol is the window through which one looks out, yet, which, by framing the outside within a structure of interiority, conditions the object by the subject. What one looks out toward turns out to be a form of oneself. In Mallarmé's "Les Fenêtres" ("The Windows"), this experience results in an epiphany of the subject, who at the climax, pressed against his hospital room window exclaims: "Je me mire et me vois ange!" ("I mirror myself and see myself as an angel"). Not dissimilarly the sky or heaven, being dead in itself ("Le Ciel est mort"), becomes a mirror for poetic subjectivity in "L'Azure." And a similar transfiguration of self takes place with the symbol of the mirror in "Hérodiade."

Mallarmé's own definition of the symbol unmistakably emphasizes the primacy of subjective impressions ("états d'âme") over objective facts. Essential to the poetic experience is the impression of the subject that it creates what it contemplates. This makes for a contrast with Parnassian poetics: "the Parnassians take the thing entirely and show it; they thereby miss the mystery; they deprive the mind of the delicious joy of believing that it creates" ("les Parnassiens, eux, prennent la chose entièrement et la montrent: par là ils manquent de mystère; ils retirent aux esprits cette joie délicieuse de croire qu'ils créent").[6] Mallarmé goes on to define the symbol in terms of the mystery which subordinates the object to the subjective state that either evokes the object or is itself suggested by the object:

> *To name* an object is to suppress three quarters of the enjoyment of the poem that consists in divining little by little: to suggest it, that's the dream. The perfect use of this mystery constitutes the symbol: to evoke an object little by little in order to show a state of mind or inversely to choose an object and extract from it a state of mind, by a series of decipherings.
>
> *Nommer* un objet, c'est supprimer les trois quarts de la jouissance du poëme qui est faite de deviner peu à peu: le *suggérer,* voilà le rêve. C'est le parfait usage de ce mystère qui constitue le symbole : évoquer petit à petit un objet pour montrer un état d'âme, ou, inversement, choisir un objet et en dégager un état d'âme, par une série de déchiffrements. ("Réponses à Jules Huret," 869).

Clearly the object or referent is only an expedient or an occasion for the subjective state induced by it, which constitutes the effect of the symbol.

---

6 "Réponses à Jules Huret," in "Enquête sur l'évolution littéraire" (1891), *Œuvres complètes* (1945), 869.

And yet, the symbolist poetic, in concentrating on subjective impressions, paradoxically erases the subject! As Mallarmé writes in "La Musique et les Lettres," for literature it is necessary to "suppress the Mister who remains writing it" ("supprimer le Monsieur qui reste en l'écrivant," 657). The two states of language envisaged by Mallarmé's poetics involve, first, the impure state of being bound up with the world anterior to language and with its desires and utilities and, second, the autonomous order of language itself, a world that language *produces*. Such a conception of language is based on a metaphysical experience.[7] Not only is the real world—the world that is real for human subjects—produced by language. Mallarmé goes so far as to affirm that literature alone exists, to the exclusion of everything else: "yes, the literature exists, if one wishes, alone, to the exclusion of all else" ("Oui, que la Littérature existe et, si l'on veut, seule, à l'exception de tout," "La Musique et les Lettres," 646).[8]

In such passages, Mallarmé reverses his normally secular outlook admitting the objective world investigated by science as the true reality, while poetic perception is relegated to the realm of fiction, however glorious. He intuits the imaginative status of the real itself once we jettison the artificial abstraction separating subjects and objects. The latter viewpoint has been the epistemological frame of modern culture driven by the astonishing advance of science and technology since the seventeenth century. It has, however, fallen into crisis in postmodern times. We can no longer ignore the artificiality of separating subjects and objects. This recognition sets the subjective reality experienced through poetry on an equal footing with objective modes of ascertaining the real. It makes poetic perception emerge as an original access to truth and a sort of absolute revelation of the real.

There seems, however, to be a glaring contradiction between the subjective thrust of symbolist poetics and Mallarmé's emphasis on the objective autonomy of words operating on their own initiative, even to the extent of eliminating the human subject, which he indicates must be evacuated entirely. To address this apparent contradiction, I suggest that the emptying or evacuation of subjectivity means that it is no longer to be found anywhere in the world of objects because it has become a principle underlying the world as a whole, conferring an emotional coloring on every feature of the world. Subjectivity has become transcendental and is made invisible on an objective plane. It no longer takes shape as any discrete object within the world. Analogously, a

---

[7] Raymond Queneau, "La poésie au XXe siècle," in Queneau, ed., *Histoire des littératures*, vol. III (Paris: Gallimard, 1968), 962.

[8] The manuscript for Mallarmé's speech in Oxford and Cambridge reads "à l'exclusion de tout" in place of "à l'exception de tout."

world of dream is entirely subject to the dreamer's sensibility, which, however, is seen nowhere as such because it is everywhere. Thus, in presupposing a world without *a* subject, Mallarmé's symbolist poetics presents a world that has been completely subjectivized in its totality. Correlatively, what we ordinarily take to be the objective world is undermined in its presumption of being the one true reality. So far from existing independently of the subject, the objective world is exposed as produced and projected by the subject through its ineluctable cognitive filters and epistemological frameworks as a priori conditions of the possibility of knowing.[9] The symbol, in effect, as deployed by Mallarmé, de-objectifies the world.

---

9 This vocabulary, of course, is the legacy of the critical philosophy of Immanuel Kant (1724–1804) and its "Copernican revolution."

Chapter 4

MALLARMÉ'S NEGATIVE POETICS OF DE-OBJECTIFICATION THROUGH THE SYMBOL

Language *per se* tends to objectify. By producing a finite object such as the word, language seems to represent whatever it happens to represent as also a finite object. For example, the word "space" creates a sort of illusion that space is an object that can be comprehended within finite limits like the series of five letters that names it. Since it can be named with a word, it seems to be an isolable, individuated thing, just like an elm tree or Socrates. These things are discrete individuals that can be designated by uttering the names "elm tree" or "Socrates." This one-to-one correspondence becomes the implied model for the ontology of whatever can be named.

Language totalizes things and fosters the illusion that we are able to comprehend them, whereas any actually existing thing is an inexhaustible plenum with an infinity of qualities appearing non-stop in different degrees and in various relations. The name names the thing as a whole and calls it into presence. But, in actual sensory perception, a thing can be perceived only in certain facets and aspects of its being at any one time, while its total being remains inevitably unperceived and so absent from consciousness.

The poetry of the *symbolistes* tries to reverse this inexorable tendency of language to objectify: their poetry attempts rather to make language dismantle the objective order of things. It is this objective order that is fictitious, after all, as the symbolist poet's visionary eye immediately perceives. For this purpose, the poet may distance—as well as presence—objects and may even undertake to annihilate them as objective entities altogether. This can be seen, for example, in the poems examined in Chapter 2, emblematically in the "Sonnet en x." Of course, *symboliste* art in its mission to outmaneuver and escape conventional structures of language can only come after, and supervene upon, an onto-linguistic structuration of a world already created by linguistic and cultural practices. The latter is the prosaic, positivistic world of the everyday (*non*)experience of things: they are fixed in their structure only by mental habit and inertia. Impressionist painting can be seen as analogous in its will to dissolve the objective order of things precisely in order to be true to subjective perception and actual lived experience. One finds this style in its emergence, incipiently, in Édouard Manet (1832–83) and exemplarily in his intimate portrait of his bosom friend Mallarmé (see Frontispiece). Painting fleeting impressions that disclose the perception of a deeper reality for the subject than this purely external, positivistic world can undermine the common-sense idea of the world as consisting in solid objects.

The poetry of Mallarmé strives in every way to avoid objectification or reification. It would inhabit, instead, the in-between space of pure activity of creation, which de-solidifies the created universe and presents in its stead a "hyperbole," an enlarged dimension of representation or, better, poetic recreation. This makes poetry insular, a separate reality, and yet Mallarmé allegorically insists on its intricate connection with a literal, physical reality that unfolds in silence. He works these ideas out suggestively in his lyric paradoxically entitled "Prose *pour des Esseintes*," the first word of which is "Hyperbole!" occurring as an exclamation. A hyperbolic expansiveness is constitutive of symbolist poetics. It can be emblematized by a blossoming flower as it expands without words beyond itself. Without rational, verbal control, the symbol is unlimited and becomes gigantic.

"Prose"

Oui, dans une île que l'air charge
De vue et non de visions
Toute fleur s'étalait plus large
Sans que nous en devisions.

Yes, on an island that the air charges
With sight and not with visions
Every flower expanded larger
Without our talking about it.

Mallarmé's poetics is expressed ironically as a "prose"—a term used in the Latin liturgy for rhymed hymns without meter. Poetry for him is a religious ritual that "shoots over" (*hyper-bole*) literal meaning. It is ideally without ordinary "vision" or common speech but affords insight into a deeper reality. It adheres to and allegorizes an expanded, unconscious reality.

MALLARMÉ'S NEGATIVE POETICS OF DE-OBJECTIFICATION   61

Poetic consciousness splits reflectively in two ("Nous fûmes deux, je le maintiens"), with an "I" ("je") and its "sister" ("soeur"), and this double consciousness or "unconsciousness" deepens ("notre double / Inconscience approfondit") as the usual authority of the rational self is "troubled" ("L'ère d'autorité se trouble") by what appears as an erotic awakening within the psyche. It can be symbolized by prodigiously dilating flowers.

> Gloire du long désir, Idées
> Tout en moi s'exaltait de voir
> La famille des iridées
> Surgir à ce nouveau devoir,
>
> Mais cette soeur sensée et tendre
> Ne porta son regard plus loin
> Que sourire et, comme à l'entendre
> J'occupe mon antique soin.
>
> Glory to the long desire, Ideas
> Everything in me was exalted seeing
> The family of irises
> Rise up to this new duty,
>
> But this sensible and tender sister
> Bore her regard no further than
> To smile, and realizing this
> I returned to my old care.

The doubleness in poetic creation of desire and ideas ("désir, Idées"), is calligrammatically repeated in the first line quoted above, with the irises ("des iridées") in which desire (*dés ir*) and ideas (*idées*) fuse and blossom. These stanzas record a dialogue between a male teacher desiring to become a lover and a female pupil being inseminated by his ideas. The moment of crisis or plenitude at the height of day ("midi"), when "everything in me was exalted" ("Tout en moi s'exaltait"), is not received erotically by the female counterpart, the "sister sensible and tender" ("Mais cette soeur sensée et tender"). She does not look further ("Ne porta son regard plus loin") but takes it all simply as an intellectual lesson, ignoring the many levels of meaning in the floral swelling of many lilies whose stem reached beyond the reasoning powers of master and pupil ("Que de lis multiples la tige / Grandissait trop pour nos raisons").

The poem has been inscribed convincingly into the literature of preciosity from medieval to modern tradition that would metaphorically transfigure erotic content because of an inability to face the carnal implications of love with equanimity.[1] The "child" "abdicates" her "ecstasy" ("L'enfant abdique son extase") in favor of already familiar paths of erudition and pronounces the word "Anastase," a name for a pope, not to say prudery, but literally meaning "rises up." She has refused to receive or even to recognize the erotic desire literally surging up from her master and thereby buries beauty—herself as pulchritude or attractiveness, "Pulchérie"—covered and hidden by the too great gladiolus flower ("Caché par le trop grand glaïeul") of metaphor, even before any sepulcher can boast of her or laugh ("Avant qu'un sepulcher ne rie"). Modern poetic creation is analyzed here as driven by a certain Narcissistic split into lover and learner, master and maid, that fails to consummate but rather sublimates desire and produces the poem. As revealed here by Mallarmé's "ars poetica," a theoretical detour and dissembling turns out to be constitutive of poetic creativity.

The symbol is taken not as the terminal object of reference for language in a symbolic poem but rather as a sort of lens for focusing a much larger field of perception. In fact, symbolic perception opens up or transforms its objects so that they are no longer objects but rather merely heuristic devices for channeling the act of perception, which may be considered an act of the subject. And whether there is any object whatsoever in perception becomes a moot point. The important point is the freedom of the perceiving act itself, which remains perhaps freer by not directly confronting any sort of objectivity or given fact of the matter at all. Certain Romantics expressed this revolution in perception early on as "seeing the infinite in all things," to cite Blake's *Marriage of Heaven and Hell*. Blake admitted that his visions did not consist in "any finite organical perception." And yet Mallarmé peaks beyond the metaphorical veil, the fig leaf (or gladiolus) of his poem, at the finite distended organ, his "long désir," as silently conditioning the most extravagant and free of poetic fantasies.

Historically, symbolism presents itself when a need to open up other channels of meaning besides those recognized by scientific positivism comes to be strongly felt at various stages of the industrial revolution.[2] Thus symbolist meaning defines itself against denotative, scientific, pragmatic

---

1 Walter Fowlie, *Mallarmé* (Chicago: University of Chicago Press, 1953), 200–09.
2 Edmund Wilson, *Axel's Castle: A Study in the Imaginative Literature of 1870–1930* (New York: Charles Scribner's Sons, 1959 [1931]), 268, develops a classic account of this motivation and provenance of the broader symbolist tradition of Yeats, Valéry, Eliot, Proust, Joyce, Stein.

meaning in language. And yet an indescribable, literal rootedness of language in physiological fact (his distended organ) is acknowledged by Mallarmé's speaker, but only as a disappearing source of poetic creation. This origin outside language is unretrievable for the poem and its language. Still, it can be compensated for from within language by the unlimited constructions and productions of fantasy.

The emptiness of language resulting from its merely representing an absent object, what we may term its objective emptiness, makes it open to every sort of subjective in-pouring of contents to fill it out. What is missing on the objective side constitutes an opportunity for investment on the subjective side. It is not surprising that the *symbolistes* discovered one of their richest symbols in the "cygne"—which means "swan," but also homophonically says "sign" ("signe"). This word in French symbolist poetry, starting with Baudelaire and Mallarmé, intimates the transfiguration of the pure, blank linguistic sign, "white" like the swan, into an inexhaustible wealth of associations to be made by individuals and their subjective fantasies. As an open, indeterminate or omni-determinable sign, the "symbol" thus becomes itself a source of perceptions, a verbal unity containing a universe. The whole of the universe comes to be experienced more essentially as an inner world.

Mallarmé's poetics are known especially for their elimination of any referent external to the poem. A characteristic imagery developed by Mallarmé from beginning to end of his poetic *oeuvre* figures this linguistic operation. The frequent topos of a shipwreck leaving nothing but a foamy trace frames his *Poésies* in their definitive edition (Édition Deman, 1899) finalized by Mallarmé just before his death in 1898. The collection begins with: "Nothing, this foam, virgin verse" ("Rien, cette écume, vierge vers") in "Salut" and ends with: "A ruin blessed by a thousand foams" ("Une ruine, par mille écumes bénis") in "Mes bouquins refermés sur le nom de Paphos." The same imagery governs Mallarmé's sketch or fragment of his *grand oeuvre* ("Un coup de dés"), with its hint that the poem is the aftermath of the disappearance of its own subject beneath an ocean of forgetfulness. The phrase "les écumes originelles" ("the original foamings") from *Coup de dés* suggests that the poem originates with the trace of an external reality always already vanished and sunken. This absence is present from the poem's beginning and maybe even as the condition or consequence of its beginning.

This sort of erasure of the extra-literary referent characteristic of Mallarmé's poetics becomes a leading theme of his poetry. As a fundamental aspect of Mallarme's poetry, it works essentially on the logic of language as a trace, and it is what lends itself so well to Derrida's type of analysis in *Dissémination,* devoted in good part to reading Mallarmé and to teasing out the ways in which his poetry evidences the role of language as trace of a vanished origin.³

Important, however, is that this maneuver on Mallarmé's part is *not* designed finally to isolate the poem from reality. The procedure more nearly resembles a vacuuming of all of reality *into* the poem, which is a pure ideality. In Mallarmé, the symbolist poem becomes not merely a *pars pro toto*, a microcosm of the universe: it reinvents the universe through its own positing and fashioning, lending it sense. Although Mallarmé could never totally eliminate the factor of chance from his art, his consummate works approximated autonomous universes brought to the absolute presence of consciousness in pure poetry. In a certain Cartesian tradition of self-reflection, Mallarmé's cultivation of ambiguity brings us back always to the signifying act itself rather than letting us come to rest statically in signified objects.

Mallarmé's ambiguities do not simply open up further possible meanings: they make meaning itself into pure possibility, pure projection from an autonomous linguistic structure. Still, "Prose *pour des Esseintes*" has revealed how the poetic operation remains refracted from and grounded on some concrete, literal reality (such as an extended phallus) that it cannot directly represent. For Mallarmé, often this is an unmasterable erotic desire or mis/adventure, as in the case of the faun most conspicuously. The fact that the words were able to support one interpretation turns out not to depend on the actual existence of anything referred to by that interpretation. This becomes evident once it is discovered that the words might also mean something totally different without any verifiable change to whatever may exist or is the case externally.

An exemplary poem in this regard is "A la nue accablante tu" ("Silenced by the crushing cloud"), the imagery of which effectively condenses "Un coup de dés" into a few lines. This poem makes its "sepulchral shipwreck" ("sépulcral naufrage") doubly ambiguous by flowing into a description of what is ostensibly another event, the drowning of an infant siren.⁴ This semantic drift casts a sort of indeterminacy over the event itself, which has in any case disappeared, leaving only traces, which are thereby absolutized since there is no event in itself outside them to which the poem can refer and be anchored.

---

3 Derrida, "La double séance," in *La dissémination* (Paris: Seuil, 1972), 215–346. See, further, Barnaby Norman, *Mallarmé's Sunset: Poetry at the End of Time* (Leeds: Leggenda, 2014), 97–138.

4 Jacques Rancière, *Mallarmé. La politique de la sirène* (Paris: Hachette 1996), 15–20, pursues this image and the scene it condenses and implies in opening his reading of the poet.

The trace is no longer to be interpreted by reference to something else but rather projects the referent out of itself.

Mallarmé's ambiguities serve to dissolve our assumption that things are said in a certain way because that is how they are. The way they are said is absolutized by the ambiguity: it does not depend on anything except itself, with its own intrinsic possibilities. And the possible referents become aleatory, derivative projections. This constitutes a reversal of a certain common-sense notion that *how* a thing is said does not matter so long as it is clear *what* thing is being said. Poetry is the sort of language in which this assumption most obviously does not hold, and this may be said of Mallarmé's poetry in the highest degree. The astonishing power of Mallarmé's use of ambiguity convinces the reader, who experiences delight in the brilliant shimmer and unfathomability of an undecidable phrase, that indeed the poetic meaning is something altogether greater than any mere thing or potential referent could be. Poetry has thus created an altogether superior reality. This "complément supérieur," in the phrase of "Crise de vers," is demonstrated in perhaps its most seductive manner by Mallarmé's "L'après-midi d'un faune." We can now return to and complete our reading of this poem in an ontological register projecting it onto a higher speculative plane. Of course, we have only alluded to Mallarmé's major work and have given only suggestive readings of a few select samples of other poems, but my hope is that these illuminations allow the lineaments and motivations of his original and earth-shattering poetics to be discerned.

"L'après-midi d'un faune" Encore: From Representational Emptying to Verbal Presence

A titillating example and a consummate performance of the synergistic ambiguity that characterizes Mallarmé's poetry is the faun's opening statement: "Ces nymphes, je les veux perpétuer" ("These nymphs, I want to perpetuate them"). The aptness of this phrase might be explained by its capturing an ambivalence within the psychology of the faun, who desires the nymphs as aesthetic objects for his poetic art of piping but also as sexual objects with whom to engender progeny. They are eternalized in the poem he creates about them. Yet they could also be "perpetuated," at least in the faun's fantasy, by sexual reproduction. In this manner, the complexity of the real (psychological) situation of the faun would be subtly matched by a semantically complicated use of the word "perpétuer."

Certainly, this much is true at the semantic level and has its effectiveness. But the fact that the word has this power of suggestiveness gives it a density, a presence, a puissance of its own apart from any determinate references.

The surface shimmer of the word on its own becomes a sensual plenum, inexhaustible in itself even apart from its value as a sign of something else. The word works as an ideational essence some of whose resources are manifest in its ambiguous meanings but whose ideality is not constituted merely by reference to specific objects. Its meaning is made vastly richer by proliferating connotations through all manner of symbolic connections. For example, the phonetic energies of the explosive "p" and "t" sounds in "perpétuer" are, in this context, explosively and evocatively erotic.

The faun asks whether he has loved a dream ("Aimai-je un rêve?"). When doubting whether he has only imagined himself as the lover of these enticing nymphs, the faun is as tormented by doubt as is Descartes. And yet, this doubt itself has something enticing about it and fulfills itself in subtle branchings ("s'achève / En maint rameau subtil"). Whether they are a dream or not, the nymphs are certainly *significant* as objects of his desire. By being signified, they are at least real as language, irrespective of their referential reality, which only further determines this significance in a matter-of-fact way. Even if they are real, the faun really loves only his linguistically determined and meaningful image of them. This, however, is regrettable ("hélas") since then he has only offered to himself in solitude what he describes, in a self-congratulatory mode, as a gallant triumph: it becomes merely "the *ideal* fault of roses" ("la faute idéale de roses"). In fact, by means of language—here the language of courtly love—the faun makes himself solitary and makes the outer world of reference unreal.

The faun takes recourse (like Descartes) to reflection: "Refléchissons ..." ("Let's reflect ..."). His discourse is an intensely self-reflexive soliloquy, a poetry of meditation. In fact, he talks *to himself* ("tu," you) about the "women" ("femmes") whom he "glosses" ("tu gloses"). He imagines them in his discourse as real women precisely at the very moment that he realizes they may be but figments of the desire of his "fabulous senses" ("tes sens fabuleux"). The entire scene and encounter at this point risks collapsing into being exclusively self-reflexive, and this predicament produces a bifurcation between the phantom and the real, as if each were only the mirror image of the other.

As the signified of a dream and a desire, the object(s) of love was (were) inherently multiple. Such object-ness does not meet the singularizing criteria of the empirically real. So the faun differentiates between one who is chaste and the other who is full of sighings ("tout soupirs"). Does this contrast indicate the articulation of a reality such as one feels in a warm breeze on one's fur? No, the sole ("seule") wind here is that produced by the faun's own flute, his art, and the only murmur of water to be heard is the music poured out by that instrument ("Ne murmure point d'eau que ne verse ma flûte"). He is alone with the *two* pipes ("deux tuyeaux") of his flute: again, ambiguity is symbolized by bifurcation. The word for pipes ("*tu*yeax") itself repeats the self-referential "tu" (you) in which everything the faun says and does remains entangled. There is, after all, perhaps something sterile about this art, this "artificial breath of inspiration that regains heaven" ("soufflé artificiel / De l'inspiration, qui regagne le ciel") as opposed to words like seeds fecundating the earth. The sound of this music disperses in an "arid," rather than a fecundating, "rain" ("Qu'il disperse le son dans une pluie aride").

The faun addresses and sexualizes nature, the "Sicilian shores," which he ravishes or sacks with his "vanity" ("ma vanité saccage"). His emptiness (the literal sense of "vanité") is his only real force and power. He celebrates the hollow reeds by which he dominates nature and makes his songs. The reeds are themselves dominated ("creux roseaux domptés") by his skillful art in playing. Out of his playing emerge in flight the "cygnes" (swans, but also empty signs, "signes," by homophony) or naiads ("*Ce vol de cygnes, non! de naïades*"). In either case, an "animal whiteness" ("*blancheur animale*") is saved or dives ("*se sauve / Ou plonge ...*"). This art of signifying releases but also enables the escape of the object, which is paradoxically the only way to possess it. Lunging for it, unheeding of the necessary indirection of art, he loses it. Too much desire of sexual union by one who seeks for the feminine ("qui cherche le *la*") causes him to miss remarking the art by which it escaped him ("Sans marquer par quel art ensemble détala"). And this leaves him to wake up erect and alone ("Droit et seul").

However, this is not exactly disillusion because it is only by backing off from the feminine that the faun can experience it in language—as the generic particle ("la") for anything feminine. Language is all general, and so also is the faun's desire, since, like the poet's, it is inextricable from desire in language. The faun is seeking the feminine ("le *la*") but cannot sustain too much of the real thing, the "hymen" ("hymen"), so to speak, that really stands between desire and its sensual fulfilment. Such is his animal ingenuousness. He needs only certain duplicitous signs to nourish his doubt. They allow him to go on with his dream and fantasy. As such, and as a mythological creature, he symbolizes and perhaps epitomizes the condition of impotence of poetry in a secular age, which Mallarmé metamorphoses into poetry's paradoxically negative power.[5]

The faun finds on his body a sign of a "rumored kiss" ("ébruité, / le baiser"), a "mysterious bite" ("morsure / Mystérieuse"). Yet even this witness testifies only through his cloven or twin pipe, which in its long solo turns on itself the

---

5 Hence the reading of Alain Badiou in *Que pense le poème?* (Paris: Nous, 2016) of Mallarmé as "the center of gravity" of "the age of the poets" ("l'âge des poètes," 31).

blush of a cheek and falsely confuses "beauty" with its own "credulous song" ("notre chant crédule") become a sonorous, vain, and monotonous line of verse ("Une sonore, vaine et monotone ligne").

> Rêve, dans un solo long, que nous amusions
> La beauté d'alentour par des confusions
> Fausses entre elle-même et notre chant crédule [...].

> Dreams, in a long solo, that we might amuse
> The beauty round about by false notes that confuse
> Between itself and our credulous singing [...].

The instrument of the reed is bid to try and return to its unity with nature and reflower on the riverbanks, while the faun continues to fabricate tales about goddesses and to undress them in the shadows of his idolatrously painted imaginings. This is like his sucking the clear juice of raisins, flush with inebriation, in order to blow his music into their luminous but empty skins ("peaux lumineuses"). He sings again his memories ("SOUVENIRS") as linguistic exercises, separating them from, and forgetting their engendering of, reality. He addresses his own eye ("Mon oeil") in its attempt to spy on the privacy and intimacy of female bodies, but he accuses the "evil" of the nymphs' "being two" ("ce mal d'être deux")—evidently because it prevents his being alone with one of them. And yet he ravishes the two nymphs enlaced together precisely by not separating them. He thereby avoids the crime of consciousness, which is to divide reality into two, subject and object. The doubleness of the nymphs leads to his loss of them but also allows his espying and contemplating them. Their remaining in undecidability is the condition of the faun's enjoying the nymphs at all. Their doubleness is originary rather than coming after the one and simple, certainly as far as the faun's perception and experience are concerned. His consciousness doubles the two axes (inner-linguistic and referential) previously individuated as constitutive of signification itself.

The faun's narrating projects his desire to realize the narrated (his adventure with the nymphs) and to move beyond the merely linguistic level. Realizing this wish would entail a forgetting or transcending, or even a suppression, of language. However, the faun actually attains to erotic ecstasy and intoxication only in and through the present of the narrative as a linguistic act. The faun's third and final inset song recounts his disillusion about the projected realization but also his acceptance of the inextricably linguistic status of his conquest and its unbridgeable division from the real. He observes that the gods, in contrast, keep kisses and locks of hair all mixed up together with their own desires and perceptions.

Mon crime, c'est d'avoir, gai de vaincre ces peurs,
Traîtresses, divisé la touffe échevelée
De baisers que les dieux gardaient si bien mêlée: [...].

My crime is to have divided their tangled tress,
Traitors, in my desire to vanquish their fears,
Of kisses that the gods keep so well mixed: [...].

The faun wants and chooses significance; he desires his fantasized meaning; but language ineluctably nullifies the reality it is about. It fixes and freezes living reality in a static and empty form.[6] The nymphs escape his ardent embrace, vanishing into the thin air of fantasy. Indeed, the horns of the faun's desire are already entangled with other nymphs, who are further creations of his lustful fantasy ("d'autres m'entraîneront / Par leur tresse nouée aux cornes de mon front"). Desire always renews and perpetuates itself eternally in new swarms ("essaim éternel du désir"), and the faun finds in himself a source of passion, a volcanic "Etna" boiling and erupting from within itself. The soul opens itself to "the efficacious star of wines" ("l'astre efficace des vins"). In bidding farewell to the couple, the faun observes the shadow or poem that they become ("Couple, adieu; je vais voir l'ombre que tu devins") and that alone incarnates his desire. The *couple* finally vanishes in the undecidability of the poem, the "shadow" ("ombre"), insubstantial like the faun's dream at the outset.

The doubting cloudiness of the faun's consciousness epitomizes a much wider predicament that affects Mallarmé's poetry in general. A recurrent investment of Mallarmean ambiguity is to be found in the word "nue," which he uses to mean "cloud" (as a noun) and "naked" (as a feminine adjective), or sometimes both, for example, in "Ses purs ongles": "Elle, défunte nue en le miroir" is translatable either as "She, defunct and nude in the mirror" or as "She, defunct cloud in the mirror." Likewise, in "Quelle soie aux baumes de temps," a feminine figure, like the "nixe" in "Ses purs ongles," is depicted and addressed combing her silk as both her "native nue" ("native cloud") and her "chevelure nue" ("naked hair"). "Nue" is but one example among many of consummate, constitutive ambiguity in Mallarmé's words. The hierarchies of literal and figurative are upset by such nonchalant and habitual ambiguity ignoring and indeed flying in the face of the rules of the logical language game for producing clear and univocal sense.

---

6 A compelling philosophical deepening of this point comes with Hegel as read by Blanchot in "La littérature et le droit à la mort," *La part du feu* (Paris: Gallimard, 1949), 291–331.

Speaking the Being of Language—Or Rather its Nothing

The study of Mallarmé necessitates certain complications of the commonly applied formulae for the symbol. What the Mallarmean poem presences is absence, and what it speaks is silence. This is because the only being which language can reveal directly is its own being, the being of language in its purity as poetic language, the language of irreality or fiction. This virtual being projected by language is precisely a negation of being in the sense of external, empirical reality. Yet this language is nonetheless signifying, and as such it is a revelation of being. Being is revealed by *symboliste* language as nothingness (nothing empirical), as "le Néant," which Mallarmé's poetry honors and makes sonorous. As he himself understands it, his poetry creates "sumptuous allegories of Nothingness" ("Allégories somptueuses du Néant").[7]

Paradoxically, then, the Mallarmean symbol, contrary to Goethe's and Coleridge's dictums, distances and absences things. Yet it achieves a presencing of absence. This is the real, the Nothing, *le Rien*, in which everything that is coalesces and which Mallarmé declares to be the only truth ("le Rien qui est la vérité"), even though this "truth" consists in nothing but fiction, with its "glorious lies" ("glorieux mensonges").[8] Precisely, this dimension of fictive making through the verbal alchemy of the Nothing (which is Everything in an inchoate state) is the truer reality (truer than the objective existence of things) that Mallarmé explores in poem after poem. Mallarmé gloriously depicts how absence is made present musically by the uttered word in his famous pronouncement in "Crise de vers":

> Je dis : une fleur ! et, hors de l'oubli où ma voix relègue aucun contour, en tant que quelque chose d'autre que les calices sus, musicalement se lève, idée même et suave, l'absente de tous bouquets. (*Œuvres complètes* [1945], 368)
>
> I say: a flower! and beyond the oblivion to which my voice relegates any contour [as in the ordinary perception of a flower], as something other than the known chalices, musically there arises, idea itself and suave, the one absent from all bouquets.

Naming, considered linguistically, is a presencing gesture, even if the object it produces is an absence. The pure presence at which Romantic aesthetics aimed in its use of the symbol is attained, paradoxically, in the Mallarmean *Néant*. Such is Mallarmé's revelation of pure, original emptiness to a secular

---

7 Letter to Villiers de L'Isle-Adam, September 24, 1867, *Œuvres complètes* (1998), I, 724.
8 Letter to Cazalis, April 28, 1866, *Œuvres complètes* (1998), I, 696.

age, even without knowledge of Buddhism, as he remarks in the letter to Cazalis dated April 28, 1866.

The absence that Mallarmé discovers to be the essence of things, and the absences that his poems *are*, so far from leaving out and abandoning everything that is real, re-present transparently in the virtual medium of language all that reality actually is.[9] Mallarmé's poetry faces the nothingness which is the essence of things, according to his metaphysics (contrary to the usual positivism of "modern man's" outlook). Seeing this nothingness in everything makes possible the vision of beauty. Things are seen in their absolute groundlessness and ultimate nothingness, which makes all their many-featured, inexhaustible appearances a marvel, a miracle, a gift: they are seen through the magic of the symbolically all-signifying sign. "Death is the mother of beauty," writes Wallace Stevens ("Sunday Morning") in his re-elaboration of the symbolist vision. Being an absence (of what it signifies), the "*signe*" (French for "sign") shows up in symbolist poets as the ineffably beautiful, blank (white) "*cygne*" (swan) singing its swan's song and vowed to imminent death.

This death of the sign is the birth of the symbol in its unfathomable and terrible glory. "A terrible beauty is born" William Butler Yeats would write in "Easter 1916," not too long after Mallarmé's death. Yeats wrote in another context but was still steeped in the afterglow of the broader symbolist movement. In becoming nothing in itself, the symbol becomes capable of virtually unlimited signification of everything that is.

Such is the metaphysical logic that has been thought through for centuries under the aegis of negative theology. God, the Creator and Sustainer, the Ground of all that is, can be apprehended by finite intelligence and discourse only as Nothing (no-thing), as the negation of all that is anything graspable for us. This type of negation points to a hyper-reality as Ground of all beyond any reality that we can conceive of in proper concepts.[10]

---

9 Some suggestive hints along these lines are advanced by Nicolas Robert, "Mallarmé: une ontologie du poétique," in *Sociologie de la littérature : La question de l'illégitime* (Montpellier: Presses Universitaires de la Méditerranée, 2002), 209–24. Accessed December 3, 2025 at: https://books.openedition.org/pulm/1074. I develop a theory of poetic language as virtual reality in *The Divine Vision of Dante's* Paradiso*: The Metaphysics of Representation* (Cambridge, UK: Cambridge University Press, 2021). See especially pages 144–48 under the subtitle: "Writing as the Concrete Presence of an Infinite Absence."

10 Ancient and medieval sources for this kind of negative theology are presented in *On What Cannot Be Said: Apophatic Discourses in Philosophy, Religion, Literature, and the Arts* (Notre Dame, Indiana: University of Notre Dame Press, 2007), Edited with Theoretical and Critical Essays by William Franke, vol. 1: Classic Formulations.

Medieval philosopher and theologian Johannes Scotus Eriugena (c. 810–c. 877) explains how apophatic negation turns into super-affirmation of God as *not* being, *not* goodness, *not* truth, nor even "God," but as more than and beyond all that we can understand by these terms.[11] Mallarmé's "sumptuous allegories of Nothingness" ("Allégories somptueuses du Néant," letter to Villiers de L'Isle-Adam, September 24, 1867) constitute a magnificent modern rediscovery of this type of "hyperphatic" negation.

Mallarmé thus pushes to an ultimate, zero degree Baudelaire's declaration in "Le Cygne" ("The Swan") that "everything becomes allegory for me" ("tout pour moi devient allégorie"). Leveraging the inherent negativity of language, and transcending conceptual limits, Mallarmé transfigures sign into symbol in a comprehensive sense encompassing also allegory.[12]

---

11 On Johannes Scotus Eriugena and his hyperphatic theology subsuming and synthesizing both cataphatic (positive) and apophatic (negative) theology, see especially pages 181–90 of my *On What Cannot Be Said: Apophatic Discourses in Philosophy, Religion, Literature, and the Arts*, vol. 1.

12 For this reconfiguration of traditional rhetorical terms, see William Franke, "Symbol and Allegory," *The Routledge Companion to Hermeneutics*, eds. Jeff Malpas and Hans-Helmuth Gander (New York: Routledge, 2014), Chapter 29, pp. 367–77.

CONCLUDING REFLECTION

There may seem to be a contradiction between (1) my emphasis in Chapter 1 on *symboliste* poetry as foregrounding the material signifiers as meaningful in and of themselves and (2) the aspiration to an ideality free from material constraints, the "pure notion," that emerges in Chapter 2. The latter is made patent, for example, in the "Sonnet en i" featuring the swan entrapped by matter, mired in ice, denied the flight it desires toward the ideal. The regression of meaning to a state of raw, material sensation seems to deny, or at least to shrink from, such ideality. Yet both elements, the material and the ideal, remain as indispensable pillars of Mallarmé's *symboliste* poetics.[1] What we need to realize is that the sensorial material in signifiers, as used in *symboliste* poetry, without the constraint of a concept (which is negated or annihilated), becomes indeterminate and infinite. This indeterminateness frees signification from any definite form of matter and opens matter itself into an ideal dimension of universal relatedness. Matter becomes metaphysically elastic and metamorphoses into all manner of things metaphorically. To make it do so concretely in the material of sound and image as presenced in and through poetic language is the genius of the *symboliste* aesthetic exquisitely elaborated by Stéphane Mallarmé.

---

1 The entanglement of the material and the ideal (and of the individual and collective) in a "spiritual materialism" is compellingly demonstrated in terms of contemporary literary and cultural theory by Nikolaj Lübecker, *Twenty-First-Century Symbolism: Verlaine, Baudelaire, Mallarmé* (Liverpool: Liverpool University Press, 2022).

BIBLIOGRAPHY

Augustine (1995) *De doctrina Christiana.* In R.P.H. Green (Ed.). Oxford Early Christian Texts. Oxford: Clarendon Press.
Badiou, Alain (2016) *Que pense le poème?* Paris: Nous.
Barthes, Roland (1957) "Le mythe, aujourd'hui." *Mythologies.* Paris: Seuil.
Baudelaire, Charles (1954) *Œuvres complètes.* Paris: Gallimard.
Bénichou, Paul (1988) *Les mages romantiques.* Paris: Gallimard.
Bénichou, Paul (1995) *Selon Mallarmé.* Paris: Gallimard.
Bénichou, Paul (1996) *Le sacre de l'écrivain 1750–1830. Essai sur l'avènement d'un pouvoir spirituel laïque dans la France modern.* Paris: Gallimard.
Bénichou, Paul (2004) *Romantismes français.* 2 vols. Paris: Gallimard. Volume I: *Le sacre de l'écrivain* (1973) and *Le temps des prophètes* (1977). Volume II: *Les mages romantiques* (1988) and *L'école du désenchantement* (1992).
Benjamin, Walter (1972) "Die Aufgabe des Übersetzers." In *Gesammelte Schriften*, vol. IV/1. Frankfurt am Main: Suhrkamp. 9–21. Trans. Harry Zohn, "The Task of the Translator," in *Illuminations: Essays and Reflections.* Ed. Hannah Arendt. New York: Schocken, 1968. 69–82.
Benoit, Eric (2007) *Néant sonore: Mallarmé ou la traversée des paradoxes.* Geneva: Droz.
Benoit, Eric (2022) *Le démon de l'analogie, ou: la résurrection des mots.* Bordeaux: Presses Universitaires de Bordeaux.
Blanchot, Maurice (1949) "La littérature et le droit à la mort." *La part du feu.* Paris: Gallimard.
Blanchot, Maurice (1955) *L'espace littéraire.* Paris: Gallimard.
Bloch, R. Howard (2016) *One Toss of the Dice: The Incredible Story of How a Poem Made Us Modern.* New York: Norton.
Bruns, Gerald L. (1974) *Modern Poetry and the Idea of Language: A Critical and Historical Study.* New Haven: Yale University Press.
Burt, Ellen S. (1987) "Mallarmé's 'Sonnet en yx': The Ambiguities of Speculation." In Harold Bloom, ed. *Stéphane Mallarmé.* New York: Chelsea.
Calasso, Roberto (2001) *La letteratura e gli dèi.* Milan: Adelphi.
Cohn, Robert G. (1974) "Symbolism." *The Journal of Aesthetics and Art Criticism* 33/2: 181–92.
Cohn, Robert Greer (1990) *Mallarmé's Divagations: A Guide and Commentary.* New York: Peter Lang.
Coleridge, Samuel Taylor (1936) *Miscellaneous Criticism.* Ed. T. M. Raysor. London: Constable.
Davies, Gardner (1959) *Mallarmé et le drame solaire: essai d'exégèse raisonné.* Paris: José Corti.

Derrida, Jacques (1967) *La voix et le phénomène (Introduction au problème du signe dans la phénoménologie de Husserl)*. Paris: Presses Universitaires de France.
Derrida, Jacques (1972) "La double séance." In *La dissémination*. Paris: Seuil. 215–346.
Derrida, Jacques (1972) *Positions*. Paris: Minuit.
Delvaille, Bernard. Ed. (1971) *La poésie symboliste*. Paris: Seghers.
Dueck, Evelyn (2020) "Mallarmé's Rhetoric: Allegorical Self-Reflexivity in Mallarmé's Sonnet en – x." In *Self-Reflection in Literature*. Eds. Florian Lippert and Marcel Schmid. Leiden: Brill/Rodopi.
Engstrom, Alfred G. (1982) "Mallarmé and the Death of God: The 'sonnet en – x," *Romance Notes* 22/3: 302–07.
Fowlie, Walter (1953) *Mallarmé*. Chicago: University of Chicago Press.
Franke, William. Ed. (2007) *On What Cannot Be Said: Apophatic Discourses in Philosophy, Religion, Literature, and the Arts*. Notre Dame, Indiana: University of Notre Dame Press, 2007. Vol. 1: Classic Formulations.
Franke, William (2014) "Symbol and Allegory." In *The Routledge Companion to Hermeneutics*. Eds. Jeff Malpas and Hans-Helmuth Gander. New York: Routledge. Chapter 29. 367–77.
Franke, William (2016) *Secular Scriptures: Modern Theological Poetics in the Wake of Dante*. Columbus: Ohio State University Press.
Franke, William (2021) *The Divine Vision of Dante's Paradiso: The Metaphysics of Representation*. Cambridge, UK: Cambridge University Press.
Franke, William (2026) *Mallarmé's Theo-Political Poetics: Revolution and Revelation in French Symbolist Poetry*. Cambridge University Press.
Frey, Hans-Jost (1986) *Studien über das Reden der Dichter*. München: Fink.
Goethe, Johann Wolfgang von (1949) *Gedenkausgabe der Werke, Briefe und Gespräche*. Ed. Ernst Beutler. Zürich and Stuttgart: Artemis Verlag.
Hartmann, Geoffrey (1954) *The Unmediated Vision: An Interpretation of Wordsworth, Hopkins, Rilke, and Valéry*. New Haven: Yale University Press.
Jakobson, Roman (1960) "Linguistics and Poetics: Closing Statement." In *Style in Language*. Ed. Thomas Sebeok. Cambridge: MIT Press.
Jakobson, Roman and Claude Levi-Strauss (1962) "'Les Chats' de Charles Baudelaire," *L'Homme*, II, January-April: 5–21.
Jakobson, Roman (1968) "Poetry of Grammar and the Grammar of Poetry." *Lingua* XXI. 597–609.
Kravis, Judy (1976) *The Prose of Mallarmé: The Evolution of a Literary Language*. Cambridge: Cambridge University Press.
Kristeva, Julia (1974) La révolution du langage poétique—*L'avant-garde à la fin du XIXe siècle: Lautréamont et Mallarmé*. Paris: Seuil.
Lübecker, Nikolaj (2022) *Twenty-First-Century Symbolism: Verlaine, Baudelaire, Mallarmé*. Liverpool: Liverpool University Press.
Mallarmé, Stéphane (1998) *Œuvres complètes*, I. Ed. Bertrand Marchal. Paris: Gallimard.
Mallarmé, Stéphane (1945) *Œuvres complètes*. In Henri Mondor and G. Jean-Aubry (Eds.). Paris: Pléiade.
Mallarmé, Stéphane (2001) *Un Coup de Dés & Other Poems*. Trans. A. S. Kline. (poetryintranslation.com)
Mallarmé, Stéphane (2008) *Sonnets*. Trans. David Scott. Exeter: Shearsman Books.
Marchal, Bertrand (1988) *La religion de Mallarmé: poésie, mythologie et religion*. Paris: J. Corti.
Marchal, Bertrand (2011) *Le symbolisme*. Paris: Armand Colin.

Marchal, Bertrand and Jean-Luc Steinmetz. (Eds.) (1999) *Mallarmé ou l'obscurité lumineuse*. Paris: Hermann.
Meillassoux, Quentin (2011) *Le Nombre et la sirène. Un déchiffrage du "Coup de dés" de Mallarmé*. Paris: Fayard.
Milner, Jean-Claude (1999) *Mallarmé au tombeau*. Paris: Verdier.
Motte, Annette de la (2004) *Au-delà du mot : Une "écriture du Silence" dans la littérature française au vingtième siècle*. Münster: LIT.
Murat, Michel (2005) *Le coup de dés de Mallarmé : Un recommencement de la poésie*. Tours: Berlin.
Norman, Barnaby (2014) *Mallarmé's Sunset: Poetry at the End of Time*. Leeds: Leggenda.
Poe, Edgar Allan (1846) "The Philosophy of Composition." *Graham's Magazine* 28/4 (1846): 163–67.
Queneau, Raymond (Ed.) (1968) "La poésie au XXe siècle." In *Histoire des littératures*, vol. III. Paris: Gallimard.
Rabaté, Jean-Michel (1993) *La pénultième est morte: Spectrographies de la modernité (Mallarmé, Breton, Beckett et quelques autres)*. Paris: Champs Vallon.
Rancière, Jacques (1996) *Mallarmé. La politique de la sirène*. Paris: Hachette.
Raymond, Marcel (1963) *De Baudelaire au Surréalisme*. Paris: Librairie José Corti.
Reynolds, D. A. (1989) "Illustration, present or absent: Reflecting reflexivity in Mallarmé's 'Sonnet en yx'." *Journal of European Studies*. XIX: 311–329.
Robert, Nicolas (2002) "Mallarmé: une ontologie du poétique." In *Sociologie de la littérature: La question de l'illégitime*. Montpellier: Presses Universitaires de la Méditerranée.
Rimbaud, Arthur (1966) *Une saison en enfer. Complete Works, Selected Letters*. Ed. Wallace Fowlie. Chicago: University of Chicago Press.
Rorty, Richard (1967) "Relations, Internal and External." In *The Encyclopedia of Philosophy*. Ed. Paul Edwards. New York: Macmillan. Vol. 7, 125–32.
Saussure, Ferdinand de (1955 [1916]) *Cours de linguistique générale*. Eds. Charles Bally and Albert Sechehaye. Paris: Payot.
Symons, Arthur (1908) *The Symbolist Movement in Literature*. London: Constable.
Ward, Patricia. Ed (2000) *Baudelaire and the Poetics of Modernity*. Nashville: Vanderbilt University Press.
Williams, Thomas A. (1970) *Mallarmé and the Language of Mysticism*. Athens: University of Georgia Press.
Wilson, Edmund (1959 [1931]) *Axel's Castle: A Study in the Imaginative Literature of 1870–1930*. New York: Charles Scribner's Sons.
Valéry, Paul (1957) "Existence de symbolisme." *OEuvres*, I. Ed. J. Hytier. Paris: Gallimard.
Valéry, Paul (1936) *Variété* III. Paris: Gallimard.

INDEX

Aesthetics of effect 51
Alchemy 16, 70
Allegory 29
    of itself 32
    of nothingness 70, 72
Ambiguity
    absolutized 65, 69
Analogy 16–17
    universal 52, 53
Augustine, Saint 12

Barthes, Roland 11
Baudelaire, Charles 1, 3
  "Correspondances" 22, 54
  "L'Azure" 56
  "La Beauté" 56–57
  "La chevelure" 53–54
  "Le Cygne" 36–37
  "Élévation" 23
  on imagination 52, 56
  "Les Fenêtres" 56
  "L'invitation au voyage" 23
  "Spleen et Idéal" 8
  and subjectivity 52
Being as absolute 49
  in language 25, 52
  as subjective 52
  as speaking 21–22
Bénichou, Paul 14, 23
Benjamin, Walter 8–9
Bible 1, 3, 32
Blake, William 62
Blanchot, Maurice 27, 36–37, 69n6
Bloch, R. Howard 43
Boileau, Nicolas 3
Book, as totality 16, 18
Bopp, Franz 15

Bruns, Gerald 47, 49
Buddhism 16, 71
Burt, Ellen 27–28

Calasso, Roberto 15–16
Cazalis, Henri 16
Chance 43–44, 47
Cohn, Robert 6n4, 18
Coleridge, Samuel Taylor 5, 70
Concrete universal 9
Consciousness 16, 51
  Cartesian 32, 64
  split 61
  unconscious 60
Constellations 46, 47
Cox, George W. 15
Cratylism 11–12, 29
  secondary 24
Creativity, poetic 62
Cross 31

Davies, Gardner 16
Death 43, 71
Death of God 25, 27
Derrida, Jacques 39–40
  "La double séance" 42
  on *Mimique* 42
  on reference 41–42
Dueck, Evelyn 29

Eriugena, Johannes Scotus 72
Eroticism 61–64
  of faun 66

Feminine, as "la" 39
Fiction 15, 18, 23, 39, 43, 57, 70
  as glorious lies 70
  as method 23

"flower" 47, 70
Form, as intrinsically significant 19–20

Ghil, René 3
God *v*
   death of 22, 25, 27, 31–32
   as "divinity" 15
   the gods immorality 15–16
   as Ground 30, 71
   as Nothing 71–72
Goethe, Wolfgang von 5, 54, 70
Grammar, poetry of 18–19

Hair symbol 53–54
Hegel, G. W. F. 9
   absolute knowledge 45, 46
   concrete universal 9
Homer 16
Hymen 39–40

Icon 20
Idea, absolute 45
Ideal 8, 17, 46
Impressionism 61
Indeterminacy 27, 31, 27, 63, 73
Individual, disappearance of 56
Infinity, of meaning 6, 27–28
   issues from chance negated 43

Jakobson, Roman 10–11, 18–19
   poetic function 7

Kabbalah 13
Kant, Immanuel 58n9
Kristeva, Julia
   pulsions 8, 11, 18–19
   the semiotic 8, 18–19

Language 17
   as generating reality 39–40
   as undecidable 40
Lautréamont 8
Letters, as intrinsically significant 19–21
Literature 21, 38
   alone exists 57
Logos 22

Mallarmé, Stéphane
   Coup de dés 24, 43–48, 63
   Crise de vers 9, 17–18, 24
   définition of symbol 56
   "The Demon of Analogy" 17

"Hérodiade" 20, 44, 56
Igitur 10, 43–44, 47
"A la nue accablante tu" 64
"La musique et les lettres" 21, 49
"L'après-midi d'un faune" 38–43, 65–69
"Le mystère dans les lettres" 21
"Les mots anglais" 10, 19
Mimique 42
"Prose *pour des Esseintes*," 61–64
"Quelle soie aux baumes de temps" 69
"Sonnet en i" 33–38
"Sonnet en x" 25–34
"Une dentelle s'abolit" 33
Marchal, Bertrand 15
Maeterlinck, Maurice 14
Manet, Edouard 61
Materiality, as indeterminate 73
   of signifier 7, 37
   or truth 10
   universal relatedness of 73
Meaning, incarnate 9
   its materiality 8–9
   literal 62–63
   and sensation 4
Meillassoux, Quentin 15, 48
Metaphor, vertical 17
Metaphysics 71
Microcosm 64
Mill, John Stuart 6
Moréas, Jean 3
Mortality 10
Müller, Max 15
Murat, Michel 48
Music 45, 49
   inherent in language 17, 21
Myth 11, 44
   comparative mythology 15

Naming, as presencing 59, 71
Negation, logic of 31, 71
   achieves Absolute 47
   of consciousness 47
Negative theology 71–72
Nomen/numen 15
Nothingness, as Beauty 49
   as essence of things 71
   its reality 29–30
   metaphysical 55
   and relationality 46

INDEX

Notion, pure 45, 51
Nue 9, 69

Orpheus 1, 2, 21, 49
Other 43

Parnassian poetics 56
Plato 12, 16
Phoenix 27
Poe, Edgar Allen 51
Politics ix, 1, 50
Pope, Alexander 3
Prajapati 16
Presencing 9
    of absence 70
    of nothingness 49
Prophecy 45
Prose 46
Ptyx 28–31

Rancière, Jacques 15, 49, 50
Raymond, Marcel 20, 23
Reality, and sensation 55
Reference, suspended 41
Relations 45
    universal relatedness of matter 73
Religion, aesthetic 14, 22
    comparative 16
    solar 16, 27, 31
Reportage 10, 18
Resurrection 17
Revelation 1–2
    by poetic perception 58
    self-revelation 70
Revolution 1–2
Richards, I. A. 6
Rimbaud, Arthur 1
    Illuminations 3, 7
    "JE est un autre" 56
    Voyelles 12–13
Robert, Nicolas 71n9
Romanticism 23, 55, 56

Saussure, Ferdinand de 18, 42, 46
Secular 1–2, 22
    outlook 57
Self-reflexivity 23n36, 28–32
    of language 43, 70
    of subject 56, 66
    of virginity 39

Semiology 11
    pre-semiological 11, 18–20
Sensation
    of emptiness 54–55
    as method 54
Sense and sonority 9–10, 21, 25, 27, 30
Sensory plenum 6, 66
Shipwreck motif 63
Sign as "cygne" 63, 67, 71
Signification, as absolute 17, 27, 37, 47–49, 71
    its two axes 9, 25, 33, 68
Silence 48, 49, 70
Stevens, Wallace 71
Subjectivity 29, 52–53
    erasure of 57
    existential 54
    transcendental 57–58
Sublimation 62
Suggestion 7, 51–52, 56
Symbol 4–6
    as allegorical 33
    definition of 5–8, 51–52, 56, 70
    de-objectifies world 57–58
    hair 53–54
    induces subjective state 56
    as lens for perception 62
    as omni-significant 37, 64, 71
Symbolist Movement 14
Symons, Arthur 14–15
Syntax, exploded 49
    suspended 47–48

Technique, poetic 1, 8, 45–50
    symbolist 8
Theology, Christian 23
    negative 71–72
Thomas, Dylan 54
Totalization, through language 60
    its impossibility 46
    of meaning 7
Trace 28–31, 36, 39, 41, 64–65
    in Derrida 63–64
Transcendence, of language 49
    of material world 34
    of subject 45, 57–58
Truth 70

Undecidability, of language 40–43, 68

V, as feminine 20
Valéry, Paul 3, 21
Verlaine, Paul, "Ars poétique" 20
   Poèmes Saturniens v
Verse
  conquers chance 46
  as superior complement 24, 65
Virginity, onanistic 39

Williams, Thomas 49
Wilson, Edmund 14, 52

X 32–33
Xenophon 16

Yeats, William Butler 71

www.ingramcontent.com/pod-product-compliance
Lightning Source LLC
Chambersburg PA
CBHW030143170426
43199CB00008B/184